Gerard

Hope you

Walk With Me Through Sixteen Inspirational Business and Life Tips

BY NYASHA GWATIDZO

ISBN: 1512383953
ISBN-13: 978-1512383959

IN MEMORY OF

My father, Basil, who told me I could fly.

My grandmother, Agnes Saranekwako, who told me never to forget who I am, and where I come from, as where I am going is unknown.

My Aunties, Ambuya Amai Owen and Ambuya Amai Rachael, who were best friends and died within six months of each other in 2012 and 2013. I miss them deeply!

Felix Dennis, of Dennis Publishing, who used humour to make business sound so simple!

I miss them all.

DEDICATION

This book is dedicated to all of Banya's past and present carers, whose work is priceless.

CONTENTS

ACKNOWLEDGMENTS

I would like to thank two sets of people here: those who made the walk possible and those who made me write this book. Some of them are one and the same.

I would like to thank my parents who made me who I am today and without whom none of this would have been possible. My mother is my real role model, always there for me. I can never thank her enough. I would like to thank my extended family who are there for me no matter what crazy ideas I come up with.

I am grateful to my children for putting up with me and I hope I do not embarrass them. Thanks to Edzai Soper-Gwatidzo and Yemurai Soper-Gwatidzo for bringing the essentials for the walk and to my grandson for refusing to walk with me – saying it was boring!

Thanks to my friends and family for walking with me in spirit and in person: Thandi Haruperi, Marigold Katsande, Mutsa Mandizha, Zolisa Marimo, John Usher, Peter Huitson, Andrew Muir, Beverley Farrar, Sharon Callow, Cathryn McNaughton, Grace Matambanadzo, Leonie Enying, Kumbi Gwatidzo and Ashley Gwatidzo, as well as Banya staff for supporting me, even when they were at their desks or changing babies' nappies.

I am grateful to those who played host to us over the sixteen days when we needed somewhere to sleep: All the B&Bs, the Thames Head Inn, Upper Chelworth Farm, Cambrai Lodge, Rose Revived, Oasis Private Care, Mrs Enid Barnard in Wallingford, Sheila and John Budd in Marlow and the Oxford Thames Four Pillars Hotel. Further thanks are due to Andrew and Emma Muir, Mr and Mrs Hancock, Charles Ying, Stella Gwimbi, Chido Poe, Bev, Blain and Cathryn and Bruce, Emily Pinching and David for dropping in our early morning tea and all those who donated in aid of Vana Trust.

I also thank the following companies and organisations – Planet Health, Thame who supplied me with muscle lotion plus all the nuts we ate on the walk, Cotswold Outdoor Clothing, Blacks, Bicester Hotel Golf & Spa, Fit Bit and the Banya team for donating to Vana Trust.

I would also like to thank Muni, Linda, Judith and Olabisi, my new friends and supporters I made while on the walk. These are women who heard of my walk and tracked me down at different points along the river and walked with us.

Finally, I would like to thank the Vana Trust team including Katy, Cathryn, Sharon, Musi and Bernie plus Hannah and Zolisa, the volunteers at the farm for supporting me in doing this walk as well as the Trustees – Wayne, our patron and his new wife Indira who donated the Fitbit.

I would like to thank so many people and institutions who helped me start in life and in business, including Triodos Bank, for giving me that first step on the ladder to start my children's home; Imba; Barclays Bank, for agreeing to open my first business account when all other High Street banks refused to take the risk because they didn't understand my business model – social enterprise. I was there before it became trendy.

Then there's Peter Fleming of The Pellin Institute, who taught me what I know about purpose and passion, as well as my tutors at Reading University and Imperial College, who enabled me to follow my dream. I would also like to mention BAAF, Fostering Network, Kids Company, Cranfield Business Growth Development Programme and all the other leaders who have been my real or virtual mentors. They too have written their stories, ideas and tips, which resonate with mine.

My staff, past and present, how can I thank you? You are the foundation of what I do, allowing me to be myself while remaining loyal to me and always going that extra mile for the children we are privileged to look after. You have repaid me immensely in every possible way.

I would like to thank Marshall Mubawiya for typing the first draft of this book and Katy Farnell for the additions, edits and proofreading. Dr Yvonne Thompson CBE of ASAP Communications who has held my hand throughout the PR maze, Getrude Matshe of GM Publishing who has published the book and Carmel Shortall who proofread the first and second drafts.

Last but not least, I would like to thank all the children for whom I have been privileged to care – be it for an hour or eighteen years!

Thandi Haruperi – Main Contributor to this book:

Thandi Haruperi had not planned to walk with me all of the way but she was drawn to the inspiring and healing nature of the journey, so she walked to the end with me, missing only the third day. She has contributed to the book in so many ways. She supported me in writing this story, editing over 3,000 photos taken on the walk, and collecting the contributions of the other walkers who joined us on the journey.

She will explain in her own words what this walk meant to her and others who joined me along the way.

I am not sure I would have finished the walk without her. I know at one point my foot was so painful, it was only by swapping trainers with her that I was able to go on. Each morning we would wake up flying almost – full of energy as we developed a routine. While on the walk she left me alone, waiting for me if I was too slow, encouraging me. It was interesting and funny at times to watch her blossom, while she reflected on her own personal and professional life.

As I wrote this book, she remained close. We went to Victoria Falls together to write my book as well as her own, but she spent more time on mine, reading and proofreading. It was truly a privilege to walk and write this book with her.

She has agreed to walk across Zimbabwe with myself and Liam Garcia, as part of his Long Well Walk from Sheffield to Cape Town, in May 2016.

SYNOPSIS

This is an account of my experience while walking the length of the River Thames from 30 June to 15 July 2014. This was a personal journey and I hope it will inspire you.

There are sixteen different chapters, each representing a day's walk. Each provides life lessons as well as key messages summarising that day of the walk plus a few things I learned along the way.

Each chapter also ends with an exercise to get you involved in the book.

All profits from the sale of this book go to Vana Trust, the charity I founded in 2004.

TESTIMONIALS

I have known Nyasha for many years. I met her when I was President of the British Association of Women Entrepreneurs, of which she became a member.

Nyasha always has other people in mind when doing what she does best – being entrepreneurial, so certainly her experience of life and tips for business are a must read from which we can all learn.

~ Tanya Hine OBE FRSA

Walk With Me is a tonic with three vital ingredients: revelation, inspiration and motivation. Since life is an endurance event, not a sprint, what Nyasha learned on her epic Thames walk are lessons that we can - and should - all apply in our lives. The book also reveals great leadership insights. Along the journey, we get a glimpse into the traits and attitudes that have brought Nyasha success as an entrepreneur, as well as won her so many friends and admirers. Whatever your personal aspirations or professional goals, *Walk With Me* is a moving guidebook for turning those dreams into reality.

~ Dr Wayne Visser, Founder Director of Kaleidoscope Futures and author of Sustainable Frontiers

Nyasha has been a fighter all her life: fighting prejudice, bureaucracy and pitfalls along the way. Her walk along the Thames provided her with clarity, determination and purpose and we are the beneficiaries.

~ Lady Val Corbett, Lady Val's Professional Women's Network

Nyasha's book is a fantastic tool to understand that success is a journey and our job is to decide what our first step is and to find the right path. Her journey is very inspiring, not merely because it is written on the River Thames, but because it underlines how we can realise the flow and the rivers that derive within us. We can read her spirit, as a woman that has the strength to inspire many others and lead by example.

~ Mirela Sula, editor in chief of Global Woman magazine

Inspiring life wisdom from this award-winning social entrepreneur pioneer. Practical, actionable advice to help you attain your goals and dreams from one who has overcome all the odds. Nyasha Gwatidzo's life of building her social enterprise testifies to her dedication to improving the lives of thousands of disadvantaged children and adults in the UK and Africa. Read this book and learn the guiding principles that helped drive her success.

~ Matthew Powell, CEO & Director, Primax Ltd International Corporate Counsel, Strategy and Management Consultant

We are all so busy these days and dependent on technology that the idea of leaving all of that behind and walking for sixteen days along the Thames is something that most of us could not even contemplate. There is no doubt that leaving everything behind for a period of time is good for the soul and Nyasha Gwatidzo's book demonstrates that. The overwhelming message is that we should all put everything aside for a period of time occasionally and contemplate where we are and where we are going.

~ Nicola Horlick, CEO of Money & Co

FOREWORD

I first met Nyasha when she became one of the first members of my SEED women's enterprise network in the UK some fifteen years ago. She has always been a great believer in women's networking in her own warm, nurturing style and she intrigued me from the beginning with her new way of working with social enterprise and the fostering of young children.

We became good friends after she came to one of my BLOOM women's creative leadership retreats in Mallorca and I realised that this quiet, humble woman was in fact an academic who had created a highly successful business from nothing and was a visionary who always seemed to stepping up to her next big idea and making sure it happened.

Alongside bringing up her own family, Nyasha has always cared deeply for children in need so it is not surprising that she has created her own Vana Trust charity where she raises funds to educate children in her country of Zimbabwe, alongside running a farm for vulnerable children and adults in the UK where they can experience being close to animals and growing food.

Nyasha faces everything she decides to do with a huge amount of determination and although I was surprised when she announced she was going to walk the length of the Thames as she would be the first to admit to not being that sporty, her determination to raise more funds for her charity took her across the country with enthusiasm and high energy.

The walk is where she got the inspiration for this important book where she shares her secrets on how to be a successful, caring businesswoman, changemaker, mother and grandmother who has been responsible for helping improve the lives of thousands of children for the better over the years as well as inspiring and mentoring other businesswomen by her own achievements.

The book is a must-read and we can all learn from Nyasha how to make our visions and dreams come true!

Lynne Franks, author of The SEED Handbook, the feminine way to do business and founder of the SEED Network.

PREPARATION FOR THE WALK

How do you prepare for a healing journey when your mind is telling you that you are not well?

When I announced to my family, friends and the Vana Trust team that I was going to do this walk, they voiced concerns saying "but you're not well." I had to reassure them that I needed to keep telling myself that I *was* well and I *could* do this.

I told the Vana Trust team I was doing the walk as a sponsored challenge so it would be a win-win situation. All my life I have tried to create win-win situations – with some success – but it has not always worked. My sheer determination often gets me into trouble and I sometimes wonder if I should choose my challenges a bit more carefully but I decided to prepare for this walk with as much determination as ever. Very few people know how ambitious and determined I can be.

With the Vana Trust team, I drafted a sponsorship and PR plan. I made a mental note of how I would like to prepare for the walk itself, deciding to walk as much as time permitted during the weekdays with a minimum of two hours at weekends, as well as continuing with my swimming, which I was doing as physiotherapy for my wrist and shoulder. I even walked daily when I was on holiday in Zimbabwe, Mauritius and South Africa.

As 30 June approached, I had to babysit my grandson, Justin Kuda, for a whole week. I am not going to offer to do that again! I was left exhausted as I walked from his school each day and then to my office. You see South London from a different viewpoint, walking it each day.

Besides the physical preparation, I also had to prepare myself mentally which I did through telling myself that I was well enough to do this. I did day walks on the Thames trails and went to recce the source of the River Thames itself as part of my mental preparation. It helped to have a mental picture of where I was going to be walking through.

I talked to family and friends about it, and received various alarming comments from them such as, "You are mad", and "You are going to get raped and murdered." I think the main thing that really scared my family and friends was that I was going to walk alone for days on end! They were not the only ones who were afraid: I have a total phobia of being alone.

From birth I have never been alone. I am one of seven children and grew up with lots of cousins as well, so the idea of spending a lot of time alone really scares me. My fears though were not that I would be raped or murdered – just of being alone!

I thought of ways to do this and decided to join Facebook, also creating a blog, "Come and Walk the Thames With Me." I thought if I posted feeds and blogged, then those who were willing, would walk with me in spirit and send me encouragement, so I would not really be alone. But in the end, I invited other walkers so I never walked alone for the whole of the sixteen days. The lesson here is you have to be careful what you wish for.

On the eve of the start day, Sunday afternoon of 29 June, I went with Zolisa and Thandi to the Thames Head Pub, where we checked in and had an early supper in preparation for the challenge ahead.

Life Lesson of the Day: The Essence of Preparation.

TIP ONE: YOU HAVE TO TAKE THOSE FIRST STEPS

"What separates the entrepreneur from others is that entrepreneurs act on what they see." — **William B Gartner**

"The first step is you having to say you can." — **Will Smith**

"The act of taking the first step is what separates the winners from the losers." — **Brian Tracy**

Preparations and horror stories aside, the day arrived without much ceremony. With Zolisa's fantastic cheer for company – I think she was a cheerleader in a previous life, we walked over one mile to reach the source from the pub where we had slept.

We posed for photographs and made the first of what would be nearly half a million steps to London. It was a strange feeling and I wasn't sure what I had committed myself to. It's true that the first step is the hardest but also the easiest. I knew I was on a roll and there was no turning back. I joked then that I had to do this, as we had already raised over £1,000 by the time we took the first steps so it was not possible to reimburse the people who had already donated!

We walked in a field on the riverbed for three miles before we found any sign of water, just outside a little village called Kemble. There was great excitement, as our first goal was to find water. I love rivers and have fond childhood memories of swimming in African rivers. Even far from home, I am always at ease when near water.

We had waterproofs, phones, breakfast and spare socks – we looked a sight. We also had each other for company to cheer each other along. We really did look like three women on a mission! What could be more healing than spending time walking with these great women talking about everything that came to mind and beside us, the river slowly growing from a puddle to a stream.

As the day progressed, we realised that there were no tea rooms or pubs where we could stop to eat or freshen up in this remote part of rural Gloucestershire so we ate our packed lunch, drank the juice we had been given at the B&B and used the open-air facilities as a toilet – luckily we didn't meet many people on our first day.

Our only human contact that day was with a white Zambian missionary couple. We arrived in Cricklade about 3pm and found all the pubs and tea rooms were closed and not serving food until 6pm which was disappointing as we were tired, hungry and thirsty. We had to regroup at the B&B where we were welcomed by the mother and daughter team running it. We were able to bathe and put some lotion on our sore muscles and feet. My feet were feeling great though – no blisters or pain.

Life lesson of the day: Feel the fear and do it anyway..

Zolisa's story as a walker:

I was so glad to have done part of the Thames Walk with Nyasha in her effort to raise funds for Vana Trust. Not only did I challenge my self-limitations in thinking that I could not do it, but I actually surprised myself as I walked the first two days starting from the 'Source of the Thames River', a first for me. Since I am not a regular walker, I thought it would be tough as it was completely out of my comfort zone. However, I was determined to do it. As with any new experiences, you learn some valuable lessons about life. What better way to learn than walking while also making a difference to the lives of those less fortunate and yet deserving children supported by Vana Trust. The Walk became for me a personal challenge as well as my modest effort to contributing towards making a difference to all children.

Once we got going, I was surprised at how much I enjoyed the experience, of the peace and tranquility of the countryside. The sense of freedom I felt was incredibly satisfying. It felt so good walking through fields, and occasionally coming face to face with cows, goats and sheep, as well as friendly strangers who stopped to talk to us. This was a great opportunity to talk about the work of Vana Trust. Upon hearing about the challenge, they encouraged and cheered us to keep going. Those moments were special as they were reassuring and energising.

I learned so much about myself during the two days that I walked but the most important lesson I would like to share is that we should never take ourselves out of the race before we even try. It may feel daunting initially, but once you start you will gain the confidence and ability to make it to the finish line and you will have others there supporting you all the way. I hope that my two days walk, albeit modest, will have helped to raise awareness about the important work that Vana Trust does.

You need confidence to take the first steps of any challenge. I definitely needed it to take those first steps at the source of the River Thames.

Making the first step is taking a risk, as the next steps are unknown, but Richard Branson's famous saying is, "just start it". Don't get bogged down in a morass of perpetual paralysis by over analysis. Trust your instincts and don't worry about a few mistakes along the way. In taking risks you will learn from your mistakes as you go along.

Lara Morgan, in her *More Balls Than Most,* accepts that in constantly taking challenges you will, from time to time, fail. It is important to learn quickly and bounce back. Always look at the positive side of failure and, more importantly, celebrate and share the lessons you learn. I see this as taking the first steps, where you recognise you will stumble, fall over, but keep going.

Rachael Elnaugh, in her *Business Nightmares,* states that to get a new business off the ground, you need to be working on it almost to the point of obsession – living it, breathing it, thinking about it every moment of the day – probably even dreaming about it.

Sharon Maxwell Magnus, in her *Think Yourself Rich,* writes that, in making a start, you need to be able to set goals, priorities and expectations of yourself and others. You need to rethink your values and have self-belief – why should anyone believe in you, if you don't believe in yourself?

When preparing to take those first steps you need to "clear the ground," according to Lynne Franks, my great friend and mentor. I like the use of metaphor in her *SEED Handbook.*

Muhammad Yunus, in his *Building Social Business,* advises that you need to start from where you are, making use of whatever skills, resources and other advantages you already have, when starting a social business. You can begin by listing the problems of the world then pick one and ask yourself, "can I design a social business to solve this problem?" Use your creativity to brainstorm some solutions.

Proper planning and preparation allows you to take those first steps with confidence and clarity. There is a big difference between proper planning and procrastination, as some people are drawn into overplanning and never actually take those first steps. Over the years I have seen perfect business plans with a hundred pages in some glossy paper – really polished – but the business never takes off because the authors are too busy shining the plan.

The first step needs to happen to change your ideas into reality.

I go for "good enough" but never perfect, as no one is ever perfect. I do not do glossy business plans because they distract me from the task in hand. I plan and research my ideas with a clear deadline for when I should launch the business. This normally focuses my mind and I don't like working without a deadline. It stops me overplanning or over-researching.

In her book, Lynne Franks talks about the need to face up to any lurking fears that may be inhibiting you before you can cultivate the soil for your enterprise. Fear is a natural protective feeling but when overstressed this can become a hindrance, even disabling. I am not saying I don't experience fear, of course I do, but the important thing is what do I do with it. I seek to overcome it so I can complete the task. I get support, I talk about my fears, I do more research to gather more data so that I am confident I know my facts. With confidence, fear disintegrates.

Preparation can prevent poor performance but you'll be excited, amazed and exhilarated by the brilliance achieved by simply having a go, according to Lara Morgan. I would agree with this: if I had over prepared, or thought too much or too long, I would never have started my first business. I would have had the time to think things like – I only have eight hundred pounds, I can't start a business with such a small amount of money; I have just been made redundant, what will I feed my child with? The list would have gone on and on, so I just went for it and made those first steps and look what happened. Within twelve months, I was running a multimillion pound business. It's a myth that you need lots of money to start a business.

Anita Roddick puts it so well. When she started The Body Shop, it was the traumatic loss of her father that drove her. She goes on to say the very essence of entrepreneurship is often stimulated by being hard up. If you are broke, you are hungry. It's the hunger that drives entrepreneurs. The hunger might be both physical and emotional. I believe most entrepreneurs are hungry for freedom and independence. They are keen to do their own thing. This alone can be enough to drive you to take those first steps – especially if you have children to feed!

Lara Morgan says business is won by those who are in the market working, creating and reacting to opportunities – not by those working on how to get started.

There are several ingredients that enabled me to take those first steps – confidence, self-esteem, moving away from comfort zones, enthusiasm, determination, planned goals, focus, a positive mindset, supporters, inspiration, purpose and passion.

When faced with a challenge you need to believe in yourself – failing that you will never take those crucial steps to move forward. You also need confidence to get others to believe in you. If you have positive self-esteem, it will inspire you to make those first steps in any challenges. The first step is the most difficult one to make, but also the easiest one, there is no going back or repeating that step ever again.

We all like to stay within our comfort zones; it is easier to stick with old habits even though we know they don't really serve us anymore. These habits might have come about as a result of negative messages from our parents; or people hang on to old habits because they don't know anything different. The wide world is unknown to them and they see no alternative but to stay with what they know. Any new challenge can cause distress as there is no safety net and the only way to avoid this level of distress is to remain in the safety zone.

I use my enthusiasm as a safety net to keep me going as, without it, I could not take the first steps in any challenge, for instance, my walk. Enthusiasm keeps you going and focused. It also gives you the energy to step forward and look ahead. It is such an important catalyst in any journey. Enthusiasm is the foundation to solving any challenge; it is a self-healing force that keeps you positive.

Motivation is also crucial in taking those first steps. The best way to keep motivated is to stay focused on where you are going and on what you are doing. In my walk, I was walking to heal myself as well as fundraise for Vana Trust. These were important motivational reasons for facing up to such a challenge.

Without positive reasons to do any task, it's really almost impossible to remain motivated.

Goal Setting

Goal setting maps out what I need to achieve within measured and specific timescales. I use the SMART Goals setting model.

In my challenge to walk the length of the River Thames from the source to the Thames Barrier, I was very specific.

I set out to do it in sixteen days, walking roughly 20 miles per day. This was a SMART goal, which is Specific, Measurable, Achievable, Realistic and Timed. I find using SMART goals useful in my business. Each year I set goals for Banya and they are reviewed quarterly to check if we are still on track and I adjust plans accordingly. Without a plan, you are really walking in darkness, and if you are aimless, you will fail to reach your goals.

I found myself in a relaxed frame of mind throughout the walk. Walking is like meditation to me. I get into a meditative zone, which I believe is similar to meditation in yoga classes. But I have tried yoga, and I find my mind wanders and I start answering emails in my head, which stresses me even more – whereas walking is stress relief for me.

As I took the first steps, I knew I had sixteen days of bliss by creating the time to walk this trail. So I focused on the benefit of the walk rather than seeing it is a challenge.

Inspiration

From the day I made the decision to do this challenge I felt inspired by the whole process of preparing for the walk, from shocking my family and friends to taking those first steps.

In life, you need to be inspired to keep ahead of the game. You also need to inspire those around you, for example, at Banya I need to inspire my team and foster carers to enable them to value their work and do the right things for children in care. To be inspired, you need to relate to the people around you and have similar values and goals. You also need a clear vision to inspire others so they can follow you.

Positive Mindset

A positive mindset is crucial in taking on any challenge as it enables you to remain focused if things do not go according to plan and it will enable you to think of a Plan B, correct your course and carry on the journey. I had to keep my positive mindset throughout my walk, as difficulties arose, but was able to remain positive and focused on the task.

Positive Supporters

Without supporters, I feel you can't do anything meaningful in life. You need them to mirror your efforts, give you support, reassure you and keep you in check.

You are accountable to them as you don't want to let them down. They are rooting for you so you need to root for them. They are essential to the whole journey, for example, on my walk some of my supporters walked with me, some made sure I was fed, some found somewhere for me to sleep for the night. Some blogged and were rooting for me as my phone ran out of charge each morning.

Everything was made easy for me on this walk. In business as well as my personal life, I have a team of great supporters – my staff and carers. They cheer me along and do priceless work because they support my purpose and passion. In my personal life I have had family and friends to support me in everything I do.

I feel humbled at the strength of the people who support me; they go that extra mile for me. My grandmother told me I must never forget where I come from or get above my station, forgetting all those who have supported me in getting where I am today. She was a great woman with great wisdom and my number one supporter until she died.

Key Messages

Taking the first steps is what matters!
You need self-confidence and determination to take those first steps.
You need to prepare and have clear goals to take those first steps.
Motivation and self-belief.
Positive attitude and loads of supporters.

Exercise

Make a list of what is stopping you taking those first steps and against it, note down solutions to the issues.

TIP TWO: DREAM AS BIG AS YOU WISH BUT FOCUS ON THE EXECUTION

"The Dream has to become a reality in an organised way, growing out of the combined efforts and talents of all stakeholders." — **Anita Roddick**

"You never fail until you stop trying." — **Albert Einstein**

"Nothing happens unless first a dream." — **Carl Sandburg**

"A dream written down with a date, becomes a goal. A goal broken down with steps becomes a plan. A plan backed by action makes your dream come true."
— ***Greg S. Reid***

Day two started at 6:45am with all of us feeling very energetic and eager to see what the day would bring. As I got up, for a moment I wondered what I had got myself into but this was short-lived as I got up and went downstairs to our generous hosts. Mum and daughter prepared us a huge breakfast and packed lunch. While having breakfast, Mrs Hopkins, an amazing 88 year old, shared with us her story of how she had just scaled the Cricklade Church Tower – all 70 feet of it – for her charity, Christian Aid. This was an inspiring story, which left us feeling we could do the walk.

Pauline, her daughter, juggles three jobs – running the B&B as well as a plant nursery and driving the local school bus. In the middle of all that she took us to the spot where we had finished off the previous day. Kitted out with lunch and Thandi with her full make up on, we started our walk in earnest. Three women determined to do our own thing.

About one mile on, we met a woman who was just starting her own walk after she had slept in a tent in an open field surrounded by cows. As we got to know Judy, we learned she was walking alone from the source of the River Thames to Goring, where her son Gary works as the lockmaster. She joined us and together we continued with our walk, resting for our early lunch in a village near Hannington. We shared it with Judy as Mrs Hopkins had really packed lunch for more than six people.

The day progressed quickly and we soon reached the outskirts of Lechlade where we needed to get a bus for half a mile, as the road was too dangerous for walking due to the traffic. We had missed the bus and were wondering what to do when, out of nowhere, a local motorist stopped and offered to give us a lift. It turned out that Julian was the caretaker of the local church and he regularly assists walkers on this stretch of the road, using the opportunity to show them the church.

Francis the Baptist, Inglesham's historical church, was a good stop for a rest. Julian showed us around and told us a bit of its history. There were a few people in the church when we got there and more arrived from Iceland, Germany and Poland as we were leaving. As we stepped away from the church, Julian pointed us to a good swimming spot, half a mile away, in the river. We had not really planned to swim but this suggestion gave us the idea to cool off after a long day.

None of us had any swimming costumes so we had to swim in our knickers! I was the first in and soon Thandi followed suit. Judy and Zolisa hovered on the bank, not sure if they were brave enough to come in. The water was cold but refreshing and so nice to swim in. Judy could not resist any more so off went her clothes. She came in wearing knickers only – not even a bra. Zolisa became our camera person, taking great photos which caused a bit of stir on the blog and on Facebook so we had to ask for them to be taken down!

11.8 miles later we reached our destination for the day and had to go back to Cricklade to pick up Zolisa's car and our bags.

I checked into Cambrai Lodge and said my goodbyes to Zolisa and Thandi as they were leaving me to go back to London. They had helped me start the journey and had stayed with me for the first two days and I was grateful for their support so far. Zolisa was not sure when she would join in again but Thandi said she was coming back after sorting out the building work at her house.

Paul joined me later that evening and heard all about the highlight of the day, which was swimming in the River Thames – what an experience!

Life lesson of the day: Try new things. The sky is the limit so don't limit yourself.

Thandi's story as a walker:

Doing the Thames Walk Challenge for Vana Trust was undoubtedly one of the most therapeutic and rewarding experiences of my life. I am still counting the benefits. It was my love and respect for Nyasha and the work she does that got me involved. Convinced that I didn't have it in me to walk the 16 days, I committed to a day – two at the most. However, something happened and I was hooked, walking with Nyasha all the way to the finishing line. I look back at the experience and I'm still stunned. And proudly so! I learned something about myself and more – that I could push myself and endure a challenge to the end; that I can walk, and walk so far; that English scenery is varied, beautiful and steeped in history; about relationships, bonding and sharing, the people we met along the way, and those who walked with us some way; the time we spent together, but also apart, with each other and each with ourselves. It was a walking retreat and one for a good cause – the children of Vana Trust! All in all, I think I have begun a romantic relationship with walking, and a commitment to more endurance challenges for charity.

Concentrate on great execution. You've got to be hungry for ideas to make things happen and to see your vision made into reality.

Anita Roddick, in her *Business as Unusual*, states that leadership is fundamentally about communication and dialogue, but it is also about having a dream and a vision and being able to develop a shared sense of destiny, showing others how they can realise their own hopes and desires within that vision. She didn't want The Body Shop to ever lose its sense of fun, passion and vision and she believed communication needed all three.

Rachel Elnaugh notes that you must remember when you think big, the problems are bigger.

Richard Branson, in his *Screw It, Let's Do It,* talks about always looking for another way around a problem, as there are endless problems in any venture. This fear of problems should not stop you from dreaming big. It's the execution that matters.

Oprah Winfrey puts it so well when she says, "You've got to follow your passion. You've got to figure out what it is you love. Who you really are. And have the courage to do that. I believe that the only courage anybody ever needs is the courage to follow your own dreams."

Dreams need to be actioned unless they are always to remain dreams. Lara Morgan's book tells us that DREAMS stand for:

D = Desire. Most people run a business to make a difference or provide a solution.

R = Reasons. You are passionate about what you are doing and have clarity of vision, a determination to succeed.

E = Enthusiasm. This is required in bucket loads in order to keep plugging on. Some people fall at this hurdle and pursuing something, which is not working, is wasted time. Knowing when to walk away is easier said than done though.

A = Actions. These are utterly critical to business progression and in most cases, speed matters.

M = Manifestations. This is the behavioural aspect of success, what was critical for her was the pride in knowing they had great products and delivered on their promise.

Anita Roddick talked about there not being any road maps, no instruction manual. Passion is your guide. Instinct tells you where to go when a challenge arises. She believed that leaders sell the dream while passion persuades the dream. She went on to say the dream has to become reality in an organised way, growing out of the combined efforts and talents of all stakeholders. So, effective leadership is actually quite subtle. It is influence rather than control. Nothing frightens true entrepreneurs because nothing can be allowed to interfere with their vision. Entrepreneurs can realise their own dreams by turning an idea into reality.

Your own idea formed and built into your company will have your thumbprint on it. Anita Roddick saw The Body Shop very much as her alter ego. I find it very difficult to separate my business from my personal life. It's my dream come true so how can these be separate entities? They are all part of me.

Execution of ideas

It's no good having grand ideas if you are not going to execute them. They will remain ideas forever.

Execution is the doing of the job, putting your ideas into action. I see this being as important as breathing. Execution puts the life into dreams. For example, a business idea, without execution is a dead business. It doesn't exist and, if it starts, it might never survive if the focus on execution is not there.

I am a doer so I don't really have a problem with execution, but I am aware of people who have ideas, overplanning and ending up not executing their ideas. They then become overwhelmed and frustrated with their own inaction.

I think big by nature and daydream grand ideas as I am a woman of extremes: I don't do things by halves. In having great dreams I do not limit myself but I make them real by turning my ideas into action rather than leaving them just as ideas.

Fear also gets in the way of execution. It is scary implementing ideas especially if they are new and innovative. You have friends and family sending you negative messages like it can't be done; it's too big and crazy and you can easily be scared by your own ideas and feedback from others. The main thing is, once you've listened, to remain focused on your execution plan.

I tend to focus more on an execution plan more than a business plan. I think it's because I am more 'hands-on' than theoretical. Plans are not written in stone though so they can be changed and should remain flexible.

Think Big

It is important to think big and globally, in life and in business. In anything I do, I am always thinking of the impact beyond me and to those close to me. We live in a globalised world so why limit yourself? In the age of the internet, everything we do is global and so we need to think on that level when executing our ideas.

I also use my values in thinking how what I do impacts on the community I live in and beyond. There is a saying, everything we do is political. The bigger the impact, the more I get excited about executing something which will not only benefit me but also the community I am working with.

Businesses should be thinking about impact from the beginning and have it drawn into the business and execution plan. Without this careful planning, big ideas can become arrogant and impose on the society where they are based.

Dreams Can Come True

I believe dreams come true. With careful execution, your dreams can become real. I am not saying it's easy, but it happens due to hard work, sheer determination and focusing on your execution plan. Once you do this, all sorts of things start happening. You get supporters, alliances and partners and they help you achieve your dreams.

Even your competitors' mistakes can become a unique selling point. When I was setting up my first business, I visited forty competitors, spent lots of time asking them what mistakes they would not repeat, what works and what doesn't. They were all very open and honest and provided me with lots of information on how best to execute my plan.

Clear Vision

Vision is all about the bigger picture and it should be simple and clear to those involved. You need a clear vision in order to execute your plan, without it there is no point of reference to ensure you are on the right track. Clear vision is the road map for any venture. My vision was to walk the length of the River Thames in order to heal myself as well as fundraise for Vana Trust. I broke down the big challenge into days, hours, minutes and steps. I had to take each day at a time and when my foot started hurting I had to take each step at a time but the vision remained clear despite the pain.

They do say, there is no gain without pain.

Key Messages

You should always dream and come up with ideas no matter how big or crazy they seem. Do execute your dreams with clear planning and vision. Dreams can come true.

Have a clear vision to focus on.

Feel the fear but do it anyway.

Get supporters to help you execute your dreams.

Exercise

What are your dreams?

What help or support do you need to execute them?

Do you already have this support?

What are your fears and how do you provide a solution?

TIP THREE: YOU NEED PATIENCE AND PERSEVERANCE BOTH IN LIFE AND BUSINESS

"Follow your instincts. That's where true wisdom manifests itself."
— Oprah Winfrey

Day three was always going to the longest stretch with the most miles on this walk, but I had not anticipated that the route would remain very remote, without many places to stop for water or food. Luckily we were prepared and had enough food and water. Paul was not that prepared though – he didn't even bring sun lotion, luckily I had some. His trainers were torn from the start so I braved myself for what was to come.

We set off from Cambrai Lodge after leaving all our bags in Paul's car in the car park. It was a beautiful sunny morning for a walk. We arrived at our starting point, which was Lechlade Bridge and walked all morning stopping to talk to passers by, some with dogs swimming in the river. As the river meandered about, we passed many gun pits and locks, which we had not come across before.

Paul became very slow as the day progressed and I had to either keep going back for him or wait around. I became very anxious about it as I had arranged to meet Sharon, Vana Trust's Farm Manager, halfway through. Paul's pace remained incredibly slow, so I made contact with Sharon and warned her that we were still coming, albeit delayed.

To refresh Paul and myself halfway through the journey, we decided to go swimming as the afternoon was hot and sunny. We found a secluded area and swam naked but this time no photos were sent to the blog or Facebook.

After that our pace quickened a bit but we were still a long way from meeting Sharon who was walking towards us from Three Bridges. We met her about 5:30pm at The Trout Pub where Paul gave up on walking and went to get our bags at Cumbrai Lodge.

After a drink and some crisps with Sharon, we continued our walk through long hedges and overgrown wild flowers. It was getting dark so we could not see where we were stepping. As we neared our destination we got lost for about thirty minutes, we had taken a wrong turn and had to re-trace our route causing further delay to our day. Sharon didn't seem fazed by this and we continued walking and talking to while away the time. We finally got to the hotel about 8:45pm which made the day very long. Sharon left immediately as it was getting late.

Paul had brought the bags and was too tired to drive back home so he had dinner and went to bed. I was too tired to eat properly.

Life lesson of the day: Patience! I had to be really patient with Paul's walking pace that day.

Sharon's story as a walker:

I met Nyasha at the Trout Pub at Tadpole Bridge on Day 3 and walked to Newbridge. It was a very hot afternoon and I was so amazed at the amount of wildlife we came across: dragonflies, frogs, toads, beetles. It really was a beautiful place; we walked past many nature reserves. I didn't expect it to be so picturesque as I have always associated the Thames with London and the heavy river traffic and industry that you see there.

Nyasha is a very determined and focused woman, she would never have given up. I have a lot of respect for her and am so so proud of her achievements and all she does for the farm.

If at first you don't succeed, try and try again

Richard Branson's tip is not to give up too easily – he encourages you to simply stick with it, brushing yourself down and trying again. You will be amazed what you can achieve. Lara Morgan believes that through tenacity and persistence you will be an enabler for things you want to happen – things which will not happen without action. Persistence and sheer determination will pay off. Never give up and never take no for an answer.

Between your business and personal life, it is a constant struggle to try to meet all the growing demands on your time. So you need lots of patience to manage these demands. Patience keeps you going.

Lara Morgan, in her *More Balls than Most*, writes about not being afraid of big opportunities, being persistent, professional and different. I like the idea of being different. I believe each person is unique, so their enterprise would be unique and different even if it is in the same industry. Your personal touch should resonate within your company.

I was brought up with the belief that I was capable of doing anything, so from this natural and relentless spirit I find I need to be patient at times when I feel things are not moving quickly enough.

Time is a precious commodity and today's world moves so fast that before you blink you have already missed the opportunity. But some things need patience and time to get the best outcomes. I encourage my carers to be patient each day with the children whom they foster. I take time to explain that children who have suffered abuse, loss and separation need time, love and our patience to start trusting us, never mind heal from their experiences. It is so rewarding and humbling to see a child blossom and thrive through lots of patience and time given to them.

I believe the same level of time and patience given to any enterprise will enable it to thrive and succeed and I agree with Lara Morgan when she says you need to keep practicing applying decisions and making mistakes by trusting your instincts and taking those calculated risks.

I push myself each day through focus and determination because I am motivated and inspired by ideas and plans. I am lucky that my work is not like work to me, it's part of my life so my work and life goals are intertwined. Life feels like a survival course which I feel no-one will complete without self-pushing or drive. It's a sort of self-imposed survival of the fittest.

You are, after all, the driver of your own destiny. You need to do it for yourself with, of course, all the support networks.

Consideration of Others

With any idea, plan or challenge, it's worthwhile considering others in your journey.

While on this walk I was full of energy, going a hundred miles an hour in body and spirit so I had to align with other people at their own speed as they joined me on the walk. When Paul joined me, he was walking at a snail's pace and I had to walk backwards throughout the day for him as at times I forgot he was so behind. I needed to be patient with him and myself in order that he could catch up with my pace.

As a leader working in teams delivering outcomes, you need to ensure your pace and values are aligned with the team or the plan will not flow accordingly. There is a need to coach and educate a team, so that they have a clear understanding of the vision so that you are all on the same page. This requires lots of patience, perseverance and determination. You need to be kind to yourself and others, relax and rest if needs be, so that they catch up with your vision. Remember you have been dreaming about this for a long time and you need patience with others to take on your vision and run with it.

Can't All Have The Same Energy

To recap: you need patience to get everyone to join and support you in any venture. By the time you start building a team you will have been dreaming about it for months, if not years. You will have done your research, even drafted a business plan so you can be years ahead of anyone who might join you on your journey.

Patience is crucial in engaging others and teaching them your vision or values as well as sharing your dream with them so that they can help you make it into reality.

It's not an easy task, as it is all in your head and not everyone around you even knows what is in your head. I try to break it down for myself so I can communicate it in simple and clear terms for others. It takes time, but it's time worth investing as once your team understands your vision, the results are great. This is the point where you need people with more energy and talent to take on the challenge and vision and run with it – once they get it.

Keep The Purpose In Mind – It's Not A Race

I have never been competitive, hated sports at school and don't treat any task I have as a race.

I find it too stressful to be in a competitive state of mind, so I built into my walk, patience and taking time. I am not aiming for perfection but to be good enough – so long as my intention is good that's what matters. On this walk great patience was needed in coordinating others as well as driving forward to the next destination.

I kept pacing myself and telling myself this is not a race. I needed to remain focused on moving forward but not clock-watching. No-one else was timing us so there wasn't that pressure. Walking is a slow activity anyway, so patience was built in, allowing us to pace ourselves in this great challenge. I kept the purpose of the walk in mind to keep motivated, inspired, patient with myself, and others.

Why People Joined The Walk

On reflection, I was humbled that so many people wanted to join me on this walk. There was something about my vision, which touched them, so they wanted to join me. I never did ask them why they joined me, as I didn't really need to know. Some things are better left unsaid.

In life, shared values and visions help make great teams which flourish and thrive. I know that it's crucial for my teams to love children and I have a sixth sense about whether people like children or not. It would soon come out if someone didn't like children and didn't value them as precious people. Time and time again I have trusted my gut feelings about whether someone likes children or not.

Key Messages

You need patience to achieve what you want.
You need to consider others, as you can't all have the same energy.
Keep your purpose in mind to remain patient.

Exercise

How patient are you?
What makes you impatient?
Next time you find yourself being impatient, stop and take a deep breath.

TIP FOUR: YOU NEED TO REMAIN DETERMINED AND FOCUSED

"You never fail until you stop trying." — **Albert Einstein**

"You can cry, ain't no shame in it." — **Will Smith**

Thandi and my sister Grace were joining me for the day. They had driven all the way from London and arrived before I was even ready. They were eager to go. We left as Paul finished off his packing to go back home. I was surprised at my own energy; I thought I would be tired on the walk to Oxford but found myself still as energetic as Thandi and Grace. They were full of beans. Thandi was still counting her bridges and gates with my help.

Grace had a friend with a boat who had taught her how to open and close locks and, being experienced with the river and canals, now held the locks open for us. Thandi wanted to know more about this as she had developed the idea that she loved boats and required lessons on how to operate locks! So they went about opening locks whenever they got the chance. I took photos as they did this. Grace was struggling with her back the more we walked, so we had to sit or lay down several times during the day. At one point we were crawling like babies with her.

As the day progressed, we met another walker called Richard who was walking on the opposite side from us. He was fundraising for MIND and walking 30 miles a day! He had friends and family with him. We exchanged brief experiences and Facebook details and continued on.

I had a theatre ticket for Dawn French in Oxford who was doing her *30 Million Minutes* tour. Before that I was also meeting my friend Winnie in Oxford so I focused back on the walk. As we progressed, I realised that I had mistimed my meeting with Winnie and my phone was dead so I was not able to call her.

In the end, I was about two and half hours late in meeting Winnie and her partner Ronald, who was not impressed and was leaving as we arrived. I had not seen Winnie for a while so we had lots to catch up on but Ronald was determined to leave despite our apologies. We ordered a late lunch at the famous pub, The Trout, as we said goodbye to Winnie.

After lunch, Grace's back would not allow her to walk anymore. So she went for our bags in the car and delivered them at the Oxford Thames Four Pillars Hotel where she and Thandi caught up later before proceeding to the spa room to rest, have a sauna, and heal their sore muscles.

I got ready to go and see Dawn French doing *30 Million Minutes*. I laughed as well as cried throughout the show. I met Dawn, by waiting over an hour for her back stage to get photos with her for my Facebook walk page and blog. I also invited her to join me for the walk but I'm sure she was too busy with the show, as she never turned up!

It was a lovely end to my day but a strange feeling being in Oxford as I was so near home but I remained focused on what I was doing. I went to bed wondering whether Edzai, my son, who had just passed his driving test, was going to get the bags and deliver them to the right place.

Life lesson of the day: Timing was difficult on the walk as we rested when needed and walked to suit everyone's pace.

Grace's story as a walker:

The day began at the Rose Revived Hotel where Nyasha and Thandi had slept the night before and we were to walk about 14 miles into Oxford. The pace was easy going. I joined Nyasha and Thandi – it was amazing to walk along the River Thames and admire the natural scenery and friendly people we met along the way. I remember very clearly meeting two young people who were walking up the river from the barriers to the mouth of the river and they were going to complete the journey that day. It was an encouragement. We had our photos taken with our thumbs up which seemed to be the Vana Trust slogan for the walk. Nyasha and Thandi were telling me their experience of taking a bath in the river the day before as the weather was very hot. I secretly looked forward to a dip in the fresh water but unfortunately the weather was not favourable. It took us nine hours to get to our meeting point with Winnie and her young man. From there I had to catch a cab back to the hotel to pick up my car and drive back home. On my return I accidentally bumped into Nyasha and Thandi as they waited for a taxi. I then gave them a lift to the stopover where I had the pleasure of going for a sauna, which really helped to loosen my muscles after that long but enjoyable day. Unfortunately I was unable to join them again but was able to cook them some soul food to keep their morale up.

I think I was born determined. I do everything to the best of my ability. To make the first step and to keep going requires sheer determination and this is fuelled by passion and purpose. To keep the fire to succeed burning within you, you need to focus on the task in hand.

I was recovering from chronic pain, so it was determination which enabled me to take on this challenge. I had to have a positive mindset and attitude to even think about doing it. I had visions of the end goal to keep my determination going. I was open to any surprises we might come across and I also needed to be flexible and go with the flow.

To get things done you need to be determined. Felix Dennis called it "bloody mindedness". There are a variety of ways to remain determined and focused on whatever tasks or project you are doing.

Rachel Elnaugh suggests bringing in fresh energy: new staff, advisers, products, anything that brings new enthusiasm into the business and its future. I do this by working at new services that we can provide, new training workshops to inspire my carers and staff – keeping up with the latest thinking and regulations is crucial in my business.

Challenges come your way to test your resolve and your strength. Your attitude to these challenges helps push your determination to see things through, as failure is not an option. This is when you need to focus on identifying the challenge and seek support when you feel it is beyond your experience or skill set.

Part of the solution when struggling is to identify you have a problem. Sometimes you are so involved in the problem that you cannot see it and it takes an outsider to point it out to you.

I always admire the sheer determination of leaders who set up companies to solve problems. If there were no problems in society then I suppose these businesses would not be required.

Recently I received some critical feedback from a supplier and I was sharing this with my admin team and one of them said, "Oh Nyasha, you don't need this right now". Without hesitation I replied, "that's why we are here, to solve problems." She looked at me with surprise and smiled. A few days later, she came into my office and said, "I have reflected on what you said at the team meeting, I totally get it and for now I am going to take on that solution-focused attitude." She said she would apply it in her personal life as well. As a mother, she feels she is there to solve her son's problems. She left empowered as she now sees herself as a problem solver. It was an interesting exchange that came out of a discussion of a simple problem.

In life and in business, you come across a lot of scenarios like this and you use determination and focus to keep going. The question at times is how you keep this determination going as it is physically and emotionally draining.

My work with children is so emotional. I cry every day just reading their profiles. I think it keeps me sane to release the emotional tension as I go along – I feel that if I retained it, I would poison myself with the toxins.

I am no good to anyone else unless I look after myself so I can prioritise what's important. Lynne Franks, whenever I see her, always reminds me that my body is the most important tool I have, so stretch, exercise, breathe, go for a walk and dance. Yes dance, I love it!

For years now I have used walking as a meditation. It's really good for you, all those trees and getting out in the open, try it.

Sometimes when I am stuck with an issue, I will take time out whether minutes, hours, days or weeks, it doesn't matter. I will then come back, having reflected, and look at it with different eyes and it normally works. Sleeping on things also helps, as you might need space overnight to think things over and listen to your gut feeling. I do this all the time. My intuition helps feed my determination – if it feels right in my gut I will focus on that. When it doesn't feel right, that's when I should walk away. You can't just have determination for the sake of it. You need to focus on the reasons and not forget to respect yourself, respect others and be responsible for all your actions. Lynne Franks calls them the three R's, they are crucial in your determination so keep them in mind.

You also need courage to remain focused and determined. Lynne Franks talks about using the courage to get started, you'll need to face up to any lurking fears that may be inhibiting you. Fear comes in all sorts of forms and can paralyse you into non-action. If you fear the unknown, break it down. What is it you fear? What's stopping you? What do they say – "feel the fear and do it anyway."

We are not machines so it is only human to feel fear but what we do with the fear is what sorts out doers from procrastinators.

I am fearful of many things, like public speaking. I would rather die than speak to more than 2 people but I have to take responsibility and lead and communicate to my team as well as my carers, my customers and suppliers. I have become an expert on my subjects of interest and I am frequently asked to speak to an audience. I have done press and radio interviews and have survived. Therefore, if I can do it, I am telling you now, you too can do it.

I do it despite the fear. I have a mission, passion to spread around and who better to do this than myself. It has taken me over thirty years to reach this point and, as Lynne Franks would say, after a certain age you become a "wise" woman. Experience gives you confidence, and courage drives your natural determination.

Over the years I have developed a no-nonsense approach. I just feel too old to put up with negative energy around me.

I use walking as a tool to remain focused on the task in hand as well as reflect on where I am going. I ask myself questions like, am I on the right track, are my motives clearly in focus, is there an alternative to this way of thinking.

With focus you remain clear and on track. Without it, boredom quickly sets in.

You can also plan ahead if you are focused as you can see things coming up that need altering or changing completely.

Self-confidence/esteem

My parents brought me up to believe completely in my ability to do anything any person has ever done. My father used to say, "if a man can go to the moon, you can too." I just used to think, wow, how can my parents believe I would be able to do that. I didn't even know where the moon was. Not sure I even know where it is today but, heh, they lived in hope. As I got older, I think these messages sank into my subconscious and I have strong self-confidence and truly believe I have all the skills to do whatever I want to do so I am unstoppable.

When everyone says you can't do this, I will say, yes I can because someone else has done it. So walking the River Thames was easy. I read many books by people who have walked, run or swum the river. My point of reference was set and I had evidence that others have walked this path before, so I never had a moment's doubt that I would succeed in this respect. All I needed to validate my self-confidence was to remain focused and determined on the route.

I use these messages, principles and sets of rules within my business life. I am undeterred by all the challenges put in my way whether sexism, racism or other difficult situations. It would be giving idiots too much power and I just don't let them get in my way.

You need self-esteem and strong self-confidence to survive in the business world, and in life. You must not be easily put off as there will be lots of people who will tell you it is impossible, can't be done, too big, too ambitious, can't be done by a black woman: the list is endless. You develop a deaf ear to these negative messages and you push on.

However, I do believe that without self-confidence, you can easily be crushed and become paralysed.

So, blame it all on my parents!

Positive Messages

Positive messages from within and outside of ourselves – they are essential and keep driving us forward. They are useful when an obstacle gets in the way.

I build a virtual cocoon around myself and I take in all the positive messages and delete the negative messages. Gut reactions are needed to remain focused and determined. I trust them always. I am lucky. I got my positive messages from birth, but one can build these up within oneself through affirmations, reading uplifting and inspiring books and surrounding oneself with positive people. Positive messages are the petrol that keeps the car running. So you need them to keep you motivated and on track.

Outcome

Having a clear outcome such as reaching a goal, helps your determination to get there. You achieve it by executing your plan in a very focused way. Without a clear goal or outcome, it's very difficult to remain focused or determined. I like to have clear goals before starting anything so I will know what it feels like and what it will look like. For visual people, knowing what the goal will look like is very important. I am more emotional, so I always go with what it will feel like. I am guided by my gut feelings in all that I do.

Fundraising

I was determined to fundraise for my charity to help others less privileged than me. Having this clear objective helped me to remain determined throughout the walk. I was scared at times but it didn't stop me. I kept thinking, what if no-one donated any funds, but before I even started the walk, I had already raised over £1,000. What more encouragement does one need? I knew then I had better do this walk as I didn't want to have to reimburse the donors.

I aimed high for the amount I wanted to fundraise so that, even if I only reached a quarter of the amount, I would have been pleased. All this helped me to remain determined to finish what I had started. I don't give up easily.

Spending Time With Others

We live in a pressurised society and are time poor – what better way to make time than walking. Walking slows you down, so it's a good way to spend time with others. It's also a good time to reflect and review things from a slower pace.

I don't like being alone so I had planned walking alone as a challenge. Being one of seven children, I don't remember ever being alone. I put this out to all my friends, family, Vana Trust and the Banya team – lots of people offered to walk with me. In the end, I never walked alone.

I always make use of any situation I find myself in. I used this opportunity to catch up with old friends and made new friends on the journey. I also used it as time to reflect on all things in my life, healing myself in the process.

In business you need to take time out to review and reflect and develop new ideas. Some people do this by walking, running, playing golf, going to a detox spa etc. Whatever works for you, do it, come back rejuvenated.

Spending time with a variety of people is very empowering and I use this time to learn and develop myself. A moment taken to exchange greetings, and find out where people are, gives me insight and I use it as a learning tool.

For example, in my business I take time to go and visit my carers and children placed with them. I come back humbled with the carers' stories and the priceless work they do caring for these children. The children themselves are my heroes, great survivors and I learn from them each day.

Business relationships are about valuing people and the contributions they bring to the team. It's all about building meaningful relationships and taking that moment to get to know each other. You never stop learning.

The day I stop learning is the day I shut up shop!

Healing Oneself

Helping others has a healing effect as the focus is on others and not yourself. In horticultural therapy, for example, you can heal yourself by nurturing plants or animals. This has been used over the years as a way of healing.

I need big challenges to heal myself. Therefore, after eighteen months of chronic pain in my wrist, I needed something big to focus on, so that I could begin to feel better within myself.

Many people set up businesses or charities from personal pain, for example, a cancer charity because a personal friend or family member has died from cancer. You are driven by that level of pain to want to do something about it and in the process you heal yourself. I find this a really powerful concept and use it all the time. In helping others, I am also helping myself.

Attitude is the be all and end all of everything.

Key messages

You need energy, passion, purpose and aims to get going.
Self-esteem, self-belief, confidence.
Positive attitude
Determination.
Reflections.

Exercise

What things keep you going?
What are the reasons behind that determination?
What makes you wake up in the morning?
What makes your heart sing?

TIP FIVE: YOU NEED A POSITIVE ATTITUDE TO STAY MOTIVATED

"The Greatest discovery of all time is that a person can change his future by merely changing his attitude." — **Oprah Winfrey**

Oxford to Abingdon

Back to just the two of us, Thandi and I walked to Abingdon. The day started at Osney Bridge after we got lost trying to find the bridge. We had dropped by Emily's house to see the triplets and Cathryn. We walked with Emily as she took David to school and found our way from where she directed us. The route became busier from Oxford onwards.

As it was morning, the route was full of cyclists going to work, and this made the walk a little more difficult that day. We also met more people. Some we spoke with, some took photos of us, and some we walked with along the way. We met a white Zimbabwean couple who later donated on my Just Giving page.

My left foot started hurting halfway so I decided to put on my sandals instead. This was the worst mistake I made and nearly ended the walk! As the day progressed my foot got more painful, I had to consciously watch where I was walking. I could have easily counted every step to Abingdon Bridge.

It was my lucky day as this was the shortest walk so far. By 2pm we had finished and realized that we hadn't arranged to go to our hosts for the evening until 6pm, so we called Paul to come and pick us up and take me back home for a few hours.

I was a bit homesick so was happy to be taken back to the farm. I was able to bathe and wash some of our clothes, eat some home cooked food as well as fit in a massage from Jane who arrived at 6 pm as arranged. It was lovely being home but we did want to finish off the walk.

Paul was taking us to our next hosts, Mr. and Mrs. Hancock who had prepared us a feast for supper. It was very humbling having these supportive people all the way. We were treated like royalty by Ambuya Millie. In the morning she organised a lift for us to our starting point, Abingdon Bridge.

Life lesson of the day: Remain focused despite challenges and temptation (bad left foot and feeling homesick).

Bev's story as a walker:

Although recovering from a bout of pneumonia, nothing was going to deter me from joining my dearest friend on her walk along The Thames!

I was delighted to take part in such a worthwhile cause and found such camaraderie amongst the bunch of us that day!

We enjoyed a hearty breakfast and set off with the sun shining and a spring in our step, enjoying laughs, giggles and funny stories along the way; even stopping to take the odd photo for our records!

Everyone was very kind and didn't walk too fast, which allowed me to get into a comfortable stride along the Thames through Battersea Park until we reached the main gate where I said my goodbyes. Although feeling a tad guilty for not having walked longer, I was happy to have played my part and, indeed, helped towards raising money for Vana Trust.

In life, one's mindset is crucial in delivering success or failure. Attitude towards life and work is crucial in the way we succeed or fail. So you always need to keep a check on your attitude. There is an ancient proverb which says, "work done with a cheerful attitude is like rain falling on the desert."

In their *The 5 Languages of Appreciation in the Workplace*, Gary Chapman and Paul White talk about "attitude check" in working in a team. Positive attitude feeds the passion and I will take a day off to reflect, visit an exhibition or conference to find new and innovative ideas to help others as well as to keep myself inspired.

I often visit my carers and the children they look after as I find them inspiring. I get ideas and feedback which keeps me motivated and validates what we are doing. If we are making mistakes this gives me an opportunity to put things right.

Sometimes it is difficult to stay positive but, as a leader or even as a parent, you need to put up a front, a protective mask to present to your team and the world. I am so in tune with my team. They know me and can see beyond the mask so they support me. Transparency when used properly can be very effective in such a situation. I will share bits without overwhelming my team, as really it is not fair to overburden them. Some people call this keeping your professional distance. Do whatever works for you in creating this distance. You don't want to be cold, removed and uncaring.

Sometimes simple things like revisiting your original motives, keeps you going and improves your attitude. This is because you get so bogged down with one crisis after another that you forget the why, the long-term goals and your motivation.

You have to introduce some fun into your life to keep you motivated. No-one does it better than Richard Branson, he talks about it in all his books. It seems that having fun is central to Virgin's core values and business. Try it your way to keep you going in your work life.

If what is bothering you is an irritation, then look at it as a great source of energy and creativity. This new energy can easily re-motivate you. I find you can create good things from irritation. If I am irritated or feel lost for solutions, if I don't understand something – I research, I read, I ask friends and family, peers, whoever will talk to me so I get new energy to find the answers.

Anita Roddick said passion is your guide and instinct tells you where to go when a challenge arises, so use your instinct to keep motivated and moving forward.

Staying Positive

Having a positive attitude towards a challenge keeps you positive throughout the journey. Having people around you with a positive attitude feeds into this, allowing those people to join you on your journey. I remain positive and my intentions are good – even when things get tough. I find having a clear vision, purpose and passion keeps me motivated, improves my attitude and keeps me going. You need a caring attitude to attract others to support you.

Believing In Yourself

You really need to believe in yourself in order to achieve your dreams. This is the first task to set yourself when planning ideas and turning them into business. You need to believe that you can do this, that it's a worthwhile venture or product. Once you have this belief, you can then convince others to join you as team members or customers. You will get lots of discouragement, but if you believe in yourself this will not stop you.

You will get complaints from customers, for example, about your service or product. Use this to develop the product and learn from it because you believe in yourself. Believing in yourself is really the foundation of everything.

Why Was I Doing This

The reasons I do things are very clear in my mind and keep me motivated. I write them down to keep me focused and remind myself each day. For my walk I had clearly written reasons such as, I want to heal myself; I want to raise money for Vana Trust. I also wanted to mark 50 years of my life with some meaningful challenge.

There were added bonuses which came to light while on the walk: I lost more than a stone during the walk and met new people.

Attitude Is Everything That Keeps You Going

Attitude is relative to input and output. With a positive attitude you are motivated to carry things through, therefore great output means great results. You get out what you put in. When I have a positive attitude towards a task, it feels a lot lighter and easier to do. Whereas a negative attitude makes everything heavy and the task is never done. Sometimes it never gets started due to attitude.

Attitude fuels everything towards reaching your goal. You also attract others by your attitude and they will become your greatest fans and supporters. You inspire others with a great positive attitude. It can become infectious. Without a positive attitude you don't have energy and without energy you have nothing.

Key messages

You need a positive attitude to keep going.
Attitude is everything that keeps you going.
Believing in yourself.
You need clear reasons why you are doing the task.
It is essential to have a positive attitude.

Positive attitude is your energy.
Others are attracted to positive attitude.
Positive attitude motivates.

Exercise

List things that keep you motivated, giving you a positive attitude.

TIP SIX: YOU NEED PASSION

"Without passion you don't have energy, without energy you have nothing." — **Dalai Lama**

Abingdon to Wallingford

The day started with light rain at Ambuya's house. Thandi did her Facebook update and chatted about training with Ambuya just before we left. I was preoccupied with my foot, wondering how I was going to manage the walk to Wallingford or to London for that matter. I remained focused and we started at Abingdon Bridge as planned. It was just the two of us again. Thandi and I were still full of energy but my left foot continued to be painful and I had to be mindful of every step I took.

Later in the day, at one of the resting moments, I wondered what I was going to do about the growing pain in my foot. The foot was swelling and I felt my trainers becoming increasingly tight. This turned out to the only time I had such doubts throughout my walk and I was beginning to feel dejected.

Thandi wondered whether a change of trainers would make a difference and asked me what my shoe size was. We looked at each other squarely in the eye when she offered her eco-trainers, which were both lighter and more malleable, for me to try. I didn't think they would make much difference but I took her advice and we exchanged trainers.

The difference was so immediate I was surprised. This was such a relief. The trainers were soft and molded around my swollen foot and my step soon changed! This solution enabled me to think I could walk to the end, whereas, moments before, I doubted that I would ever reach London. I felt sorry for Thandi, saddled with my hard and heavy-set trainers but she cheered me on – and on we walked! As we approached Wallingford, Kumbi my sister-in-law, texted me that she was on her way from Birmingham to join us on the walk with my niece Ashley.

This was a surprise as I hadn't thought they would be joining me on this walk. It was also a great blessing as Kumbi is a physiotherapist, so I walked to Wallingford Bridge with an even lighter step, as I knew I would get proper treatment and advice on my tender and fragile foot.

I sent Facebook and blog messages that I now had a resident physiotherapist to cure my foot. After arriving at our B&B, Kumbi went straight to treating me, poking muscles in my bottom I never knew I had. The bones on my left foot had moved, Kumbi said, and she showed me exercises I could do to strengthen the bones that had moved between my big toe and the next two to it. Satisfied that my foot had been well tended to, she left me and went back to her own hotel to rest for the night. Massaged, poked at, and with my left foot tied up with Thandi's socks, I went straight to bed. Only my faith in her made me sleep that night. I was scared that my feet would not carry me to the end of the walk. Every night after this I went to bed with my left foot tied up with Thandi's socks. Poor Thandi, now I had her socks as well as her trainers.

Magic always happens when faced with a new challenge. Here I was suffering from my foot and Kumbi appeared from nowhere to heal me.

Life lesson of the day: Life is full of surprises, Thandi's trainers and Kumbi's visit helped me out with my foot.

Kumbi's story as a walker:

My daughter and I had heard that Auntie Nyasha was doing an 184 mile walk. We decided to support her at the 80 mile stage. We met her and her walking partner, Auntie Thandi, at Wallingford. My expectations could not be further off the mark. I had expected to find two exhausted women, ready to give up and rightly so. Auntie Nyasha had just recovered from a disabling joint problem, which had resulted in her requiring assistance with cooking and feeding herself. Now she was attempting to walk 184 miles.

On arrival we found we had been booked into a lovely village hotel. We assumed this was how the Aunties made their way through the British countryside, lurching from one boutique hotel to the next.

Well, you can imagine our surprise when we found out that the Aunties were staying at the house of a rare breed of kind stranger, an elderly lady. This lady had offered her hospitality on hearing about the charity walk, even though she was nursing her very sick husband. She had offered the Aunties a room in her house for free.

I expected to find a beautiful country manor with an east wing. Only to find a humble terraced home. We ate a takeaway dinner, then proceeded upstairs because Auntie was suffering with painful feet and wanted treatment for them. As I am a chartered physiotherapist I had offered my services during our time together.

The two Aunties share at least 100 years between them and the only problems they had, collectively, were collapsed arches and a blister on the back of Nyasha's leg (not her foot). Wow!

Kumbi Gwatidzo
Senior Physiotherapist

From as early as four years of age, I knew what my purpose in life was and this was driven by my passion for children so, surprise surprise, my purpose in life is to care for children and those less fortunate than myself. I feel lucky and privileged to have known my purpose in life from an early age and I have sympathy for others who wander aimlessly. The idea alone gives me nightmares.

The things I do are driven by purpose and passion. This is why I feel so determined, as I am very clear what I am in this world for. I breathe my passion and purpose every day, every hour. This is why I wake up each day. This is what keeps me alive. This is what made me take those first steps on my walk.

I'm often asked, "what is your secret to success?" and my answer has always been, "I'm lucky, I was born with passion." Over the years I have read a lot of business books written by famous business leaders and the common theme I find is their passion.

Richard Branson writes about it and states that passion is unquestionably the secret sauce, aka the brand essence, of every one of Virgin's scores of highly diverse businesses. He goes on to say if you fail to understand the significance of having and sharing such a palpable passion for what you do, then the chances are that you really do not belong in a leadership role.

Luckily for me I was born with this as I agree with Richard Branson that you can't train anyone to be passionate. Anita Roddick, in her *Business as Unusual*, talks about passion being her reason for setting up The Body Shop. She was passionate about the environment before it was fashionable and she was driven by this until she died. She never wavered.

Passion is contagious. In life and in work, you must surround yourself with people who share the same passion. It is the foundation of success. So you need to cultivate your passion in everything you do. Let it be your guide and all will fall into place.

Anita Roddick had two main pieces of advice for entrepreneurs. One of them was passion. She said you have to be passionate about ideas. Entrepreneurs want to create a livelihood from an idea that has obsessed them. Not necessarily a business but a livelihood. What gets their juices going is seeing how far an idea can go.

The other piece of advice she gave was to be always opportunistic. Successful entrepreneurs don't work within systems; they hate hierarchies and structures and they try to destroy them. They have antennae on their heads and are always looking for what they can see around them that relates to their ideas.

I so relate to this as, each day I wake up, my antennae are out and I am looking for how best I can help and support my children, staff and carers. I do have lots of "aha!" moments.

You need to get your antennae out and be opportunistic.

Passion for me is what keeps me moving, propels me into action.

Passion is the reason why I get up in the morning, striving to help even one child who needs it.

Passion keeps you focused and determined to reach your goal, as failure is not an option.

Without it you are dead really; you remain stuck and frustrated and never move on.

You feel so committed to it that, even if someone asked you to walk through fire, you would quite happily do it without question so long as it was a way to reach your goal.

Some people say that a person is 'driven' and I understand this to mean that a person feels passionately about their idea, cause, product or service.

It's a very emotional thing being passionate and often reduces me to tears and I am sure it is the same for others.

People succeed both in life and in business if they have a very clear purpose and are passionate about it. My passion is children and my purpose in life is to care for them; to have their best interests at heart. This drives everything I do. I am determined to give them a voice and see that they are valued rather than abused. I want to make a difference for the children I am privileged to care for. I learn each day from their stories and become even more determined from the knowledge I gain each day.

I get emotional just writing about this, never mind helping these children.

You need to have a passion in life and put your neck on the line to defend that passion. It can be anything, but passion is the driver.

I am lucky to have had this passion from birth as I am only too aware some people are not born with it and need to learn, to develop what it is that gets the heart racing, what gives them purpose.

For me it is about survival, without passion you are very sad indeed.

Key messages

Passion is the key to anything we do.
Passion gives us energy to pursue ideas/our dreams.
Passion is contagious.
Passion is the driver.
Passion is emotional.
Find your passion and go for it.

Exercise page

What are the things you are passionate about?
What drives your passion?
What makes your heart sing?
What wakes you up in the morning?
What will you die for?

TIP SEVEN: FOCUS ON YOUR PURPOSE

"Our prime purpose in life is to help others and if you can't help them, at least don't hurt them." — **Dalai Lama**

Wallingford to Goring (via Ealing)

We really had to brace ourselves as we had a long day ahead. The plan was to walk half a day then go to a fundraising BBQ in South Ealing, organised by John in aid of this walk. So, we had lots of things to do as well as co-ordinate. Cathryn and Bruce had to pick up our bags and take them to their house in Shiplake, where we would be coming back to sleep after the BBQ.

I was pleased I was walking with Kumbi who continued to massage, poke and strengthen the muscles all the way from Wallingford to Goring.

I hobbled about with sheer determination to do the walk against all odds. Thandi who, despite having not prepared for this walk, remained surprisingly full spirited and without any complaint about the distances or her 'new' trainers. She also focused on supporting me and carried my bags and water when she thought I was struggling. Ashley was a great help too. She carried some of my food and Thandi's laptop. I walked every step with celebration.

Every step was moving me towards my goal. It was so pleasing knowing I would not be repeating that step again.

We got to Goring in good time, walked across the bridge to the station and got the next train to South Ealing. The BBQ was already underway when we got there, lots of people had come to cheer us along. It was so encouraging.

It was nice to eat home cooked food, as take away and restaurant food was getting to us. It was a bit of a strange feeling for us not to be walking but we needed and welcomed the rest. Kumbi and Ashley left us at the BBQ and retuned back home to Birmingham.

We left the BBQ for our night in Shiplake where, as a treat, we got to soak our sore feet and muscles in salted baths. Yemurai, my daughter, joined us early the next day for the morning walk, she brought some muscle cream for the knees – in aid of our pains!

Life lesson of the day: No matter how determined you are, sometimes you need support from others to get where you need to be.

Cathryn's story as a walker:

I joined Nyasha and the wonderful group of walkers for the last few hours of the last day. It was very inspiring to be there with Nyasha at the 'finish line' knowing all the effort, training, planning and dedication that went into her 'Walk with Me' challenge on behalf of Vana Trust. I was there when the first spark of inspiration arose and through all the planning. It was a tremendous team effort getting the infrastructure for the walk just right. And for this, I want to especially thank Katy Farnell and Yvonne Marimo. However, in the end, it was Nyasha who had to do the walking.

I live very near a beautiful rural part of the Thames and think of it as lush and green, teeming with wildlife. The part of the Thames we walked at the end was industrial Thames. Walking toward the Thames Barrier meant walking on very hot pavements with no green shade. Heat came at us in waves off the piles of gravel and concrete. This was a very different Thames from the one I know so intimately. Just when we really thought we couldn't go on, we saw the Thames Barrier, our final destination, and walked the last mile in complete jubilation.

The 'Walk with Me' challenge was like so many of life's experiences. One starts with such buoyant hopes knowing the goal one wants to achieve. But as time goes on the stress and challenge can become overwhelming. Sages speak of it being "darkest before the dawn." Walking through the industrial Thames landscape did seem a bit like that....the ugly, hard bit just before the jubilation of a goal met, a job well done.

Even though it was Nyasha who walked the full length of the Thames, this was a team effort and I would like to thank all of those who walked with Nyasha, organised the structure and timings of the walk, the donated accommodations, and those who raised money for Vana Trust.

Cathryn McNaughton
CEO Vana Trust

Ashley's story as a walker:

At 8 o'clock we stood on Wallingford Bridge hypnotised by the view. We could see Auntie Nyasha from where we were, she was accompanied by her friend, Thandi, who we respectfully called Auntie. We set off on our 10 mile adventure. My Mum and I did not know where we were going, but we trusted Auntie.

Journeying through unspoiled scenery heads were held high. We were privileged to be on this trek. Our journey had nearly reached the end at Goring and we had to go to a BBQ in Ealing, where we were greeted with happy faces and the smell of sizzling sausages and burgers.

By 8pm my Mum and I had to head back to Birmingham, so we left Auntie and wished her well for the remaining miles from Goring to London.

All very inspiring!

Purpose is really your intention in what you do. Pellin's teachings talk about purpose being the life force that drives everything you do. Without purpose you really don't have that get up and go attitude because you don't know why you even get up in the morning. In setting up any enterprise, you need to find your purpose to enable you to focus on what's important, what drives you, what you are passionate about.

I feel passion and purpose are very interlinked and they drive each other towards your goals. Having read and followed a lot of business leaders I notice this is a common thread. They are all driven by their purpose and passion to the exclusion of everything else. When misplaced, I think this becomes dangerous and can lead people into wars. So there is a need to balance it with good intentions.

I agree with Ptaryali, an Indian teacher who says when you are inspired by some great purpose, all your thoughts break their bonds. Your mind transcends limitations, your consciousness expands in every direction and you find yourself in a new, great and wonderful world.

I feel I am in a new world everyday as I am driven by my purpose in life.

The secret is not having passion in itself, but you need to communicate your passion to others, be it within your team, your customers or stakeholders. You need to spread the word. Remember, passion is contagious.

Larry Smith, in one of his Ted talks in 2011, said passion is the thing that will help you create the highest expression of your talent.

We Need Purpose In Life

We need purpose to guide us in our daily lives, not to lead an aimless life.

Life is too precious not to have a true purpose.

I am often asked, but what if I don't have any purpose at all, how can I find my own purpose?

I normally reply to this with lots of questions like, what do you like, what excites you, what do you feel passionately about, what makes you cry? When was the last time you watched a film, or TV programme and you found yourself crying out of nowhere. What was the subject of that film?

In getting the answers to the above, nine out of ten people have the same topic and normally there is something. Is that subject the purpose in that person's life?

For me, as you know already, my purpose is children. I have the same answers to the above.

Key Messages
Find your purpose in life.
Purpose is your guide.
It's your reason to live.

Exercise

Do you have a purpose, if not, how can you go about finding it?

What is your purpose?

What are the reasons for your purpose?

TIP EIGHT: IT'S ALL ABOUT RELATIONSHIPS BOTH IN LIFE AND BUSINESS

"*Remember that the best relationship is one in which your love for each other exceeds your need for each other.*" — **Dalai Lama**

Goring to Sonning

The original plan was to walk from Goring to Caversham on this day but in the end we walked further – to Sonning. We were joined by Yemurai and Peter on the walk, so it was great having new energy.

It was lovely catching up with Peter whom I had not seen for months if not years. Peter is one of those friends I don't see regularly but when we do meet up, we just carry on where we left off, without feeling we have missed out. Peter is also familiar with the Thames Path as it is a local walk he has done many times – both alone and with friends – so it was nice to have someone who could lead us on the walk rather than worrying about getting lost. It felt as though we had our own personal guide on the day.

One bit on the walk was very hilly – this was the first hill we had experienced since we started. The Thames path is generally flat so this got our pulse racing. My foot was much better and I was not limping as much. I was still holding on to Thandi's trainers for dear life and she seemed to have become used to mine by then.

After lunch at Caversham, Peter left to go home and pointed us along onto Sonning. We walked to Sonning Bridge and decided to soak our feet in the cold river while we waited for Cathryn to come and pick us up for our second night's sleep at her house.

It was so refreshing being in the water. I wanted to swim again but was too tired to even try. We got home to Cathryn's and the same routine was followed before bed. We had our salty icy soak of the feet, followed by a salty warm bath before retiring for the night. I am not sure if this was all in our mind but we felt healed each night by this routine which enabled us to walk the next day.

Life lesson of the day: Friends are there to support you no matter what crazy idea you come up with.

Peter Huitson's story as a walker:

Early morning July 7th – sun floods in through the curtains – but my muscles are aching from a 70 mile cycle ride in Shropshire the previous day. I am tempted to stay in bed but I have promised to walk with Nyasha from Goring back to Reading today – and if she's been walking for over a week, I'm sure I can manage it for one day! I bolt a quick breakfast and dash to Reading station to meet her on the train. Frustration: there's an unexpectedly long queue at the ticket office, I run up the escalator only to watch the train slide out.

Time to calm down. I sit over coffee on the platform whilst Nyasha and her party head down to a hotel in Goring by the river. Half an hour later all the hassle is forgotten as I meet Nyasha, her daughter and Thandi on the bridge joining Goring to Streatley. The water on the weir is sparkling. We head downriver to the east – chatting as we go. We pass through the outskirts of Goring and ascend gently through the beech woods that sweep down to the river. I always think that this is the most beautiful part of the Thames near Reading and it doesn't disappoint. This stretch is quite hilly – Nyasha's party say that these are the first up and downs they've encountered on the whole route so far. We take it slowly then drop down through Whitchurch to the toll bridge. This is currently being rebuilt so we cross by a temporary footbridge. Thandi stays behind, fascinated by the bridge construction works.

I go ahead with Nyasha seduced by the promise of cake and coffee at the café in Pangbourne. Half an hour later, revitalised, we set off through fields by the river towards Mapeldurham. The landscape is timeless, pastoral and very English. Some say that the woods on the other side inspired Kenneth Grahame's The Wind in the Willows: I imagine Mr Toad racing along in his motor car. It's still sunny but invisible clouds play games with us – scattering drops at random so we don't know whether or not to shelter. We rest under a hawthorn – and wonder what it's like to make the journey along the river by boat. I explain that holidaying by river is an old tradition dating back to at least Victorian times and suggest they read Jerome K Jerome's Three Men in a Boat.

The sun is out again as we reach the lock at Mapeldurham. We look at the distance marker and Nyasha is pleased to note just how far she has already come – it feels like she's into the second half of her journey. We push on to Purley and then get lost in anonymous suburban streets where the Thames Path moves away from the river. It's hot walking up a hill over a railway bridge.

Then we see the Reading sign and the path dropping down to the river again. The last couple of miles into the town slip by in no time and before I know it the familiar sight of Caversham Bridge swings into sight. We stop in the courtyard of the hotel overlooking the river for a drink and a sandwich. We've done about 11 miles and I'm pleased that I've found the walk relaxing and over almost too quickly.

When we finish I say goodbye and head off over the bridge back to where I live. I pause for a moment and watch three intrepid women chatting and strolling steadfastly along the towpath past Reading centre and on towards Sonning where they will spend the night. I feel a little sad that I won't be with them for the next stage of their inspiring journey.

In his *Screw It, Let's Do It,* Richard Branson writes, "communication is the secret to good business as well as good relationships."

The business world has become so humane that without building positive relationships in your area, your business will not survive.

Over the years I have read many business books and they all express how essential it is to build relationships with your customers and stakeholders. You do this in all communications you make, varying from emails, advertising, social media, marketing materials and your website. You communicate your message throughout these media.

People buy from other people and you will get repeat business as you keep in touch with your customers. I always say to my team, find a reason to call or visit our customers, tell them the latest issue and ask them what is worrying them at the moment. Offer to help them with their problem.

As a business you are there to help them – that is why you set up shop after all – to solve a need.

Even in an area where one would not expect relationships to matter so much, like a public speaking business, Carmine Gallo, in his *Talk Like Ted*, writes about creating a relationship with an audience during a speech, even if you are never going to see or talk to them again.

Some people talk about "location, location, location" being crucial in business. For me it is all about relationships, as things have moved on especially with online working. Without creating good, meaningful relationships with your staff, customers and suppliers you really don't have a business. The same applies to your personal life. You need positive relationships which are supportive. So what are the ingredients that make good sustainable relationships? I call them winning relationships – where you give and take in personal or business relationships. In any relationship I look at what the benefits are, where you can add value. I'm always looking at how I can help empower, enable and give in any relationship.

To truly engage in any relationship you need to listen to and hear what the issues are. You need to be open and flexible to enable this to happen and to analyse what you are being told.

Clear communication and not having a hidden agenda is essential in any relationship. Having clear expectations is also important: if this is not dealt with properly it can lead to huge misunderstandings. Simple things like remembering someone's birthday matters in building relationships, and they all add up to having a feeling that someone bothered or cared. It is from these positive relationships that you can get supporters to enable you to reach your goals, you can't do it alone.

Key Messages

It's all about relationships.
Build, grow and develop them.
Make them sustainable.
Make them meaningful.
Create winning relationships.

Exercise

List reasons why your relationships are important.

How did you start, build, develop your current relationships?

Are they good, positive relationships?

What are you going to do differently to build winning relationships?

TIP NINE: BE GENEROUS – GIVE UNCONDITIONALLY

"What I know for sure is that what you give comes back to you."
— Oprah Winfrey

Sonning to Marlow (via Shiplake)

Sonning was grey this morning, I was wondering if it was going to rain. Cathryn dropped us not far from the Sonning Bridge and we took photos, as had become part of our routine at the start of each day. Thandi and I were going it alone on this day.

We were on a roll. Nothing was going to stop us. We encouraged each other, waited for one another if the other walked on ahead. We told each other we could do it. We talked and laughed and got to know each other on this walk.

Thandi got scared when we saw a helicopter owned by some rich Swiss banker flying just outside Shiplake. It was so remote a place I suppose we could have easily disappeared without trace!

Rural England is at its best with the River Thames as a backdrop, surrounded by grand houses and with boats moored in its waters. Thandi got the idea then she would like to hire a boat, perhaps even own one, the grander the better.

It's good to have dreams and something to work towards. We also thought maybe we could do the same journey next time on a boat as Peter had mentioned a book called *Three Men in a Boat* yesterday. This gave us the idea and our book will be called *Two Black Women in a Boat.* The next bestseller indeed!

As we approached Marlow, we met Jane, someone I know from my village whom I had not seen for years. It was a nice surprise and one that helped Vana Trust too. She instantly donated 40 Euros towards the walk. She had just returned from France, hence the Euros. Great meeting – went home with a donation!

That evening, we were sleeping in Marlow, so we had to get a cab to a lovely B&B on its outskirts.

Life lesson of the day: Dreams can come true. So Thandi, keep dreaming about those boats!

John's story as a walker:

I joined the walk at Staines on the towpath. We had arranged to meet at a church near the path, but it turned out there were several nearby and we were waiting at different churches, but we met up fairly quickly and had breakfast at a café run by a local day centre. At Staines the path was well established compared with some of the pathways in the countryside earlier on the walk. We went from Staines to an island near Sunbury where the team was staying overnight with a friend of Nyasha's. During the walk it was interesting to see the houses alongside the river. I thought what a nice location to live, but there is always the risk of flooding. We asked passers-by to take group photos of the team and they usually took an interest in what we were doing. The girls wasted no time in telling them about it and giving them a leaflet. I think a few may have donated since.

The next day was Sunbury to Kingston. I was going home each night and joining the team in the morning. I was a bit late the next morning as Sunbury station proved to be a long walk from the point on the river where I had arranged to meet them. We got to Kingston and cut the walk short by a few miles as it was a very hot day and everyone was struggling a bit and suffering from the heat.

I joined the team the next day at Putney Bridge where someone else joined the group and we walked along the Thames Path. The riverside is very built up at this point with flats lining the river. We had a nice breakfast at a flat on the river belonging to a friend of Nyasha. It had been built in the last 20 years or so, and had views over a long stretch of the Thames. These were former industrial sites that were originally there to use river transport. I used to live in this area and had not seen these new developments before. From here we walked along the path again, mostly alongside new residential developments and passed through Battersea Park, which has been restored with many of the features from its Victorian past, as has Vauxhall Pleasure Gardens.

We were now in central London and were walking along main roads on the north side of the river although this was a part that I rarely go to so it was interesting to walk through it. We passed Tate Britain and dived in for coffee. Then we crossed the river and joined the millions of tourists on the South Bank. We had lunch at the Royal Festival Hall café and finished that day at Tower Bridge with a drink in a pub. We had a look in City Hall and found the location of our houses on the huge floor plan of London in the reception area.

Next day, the last, we started at Tower Bridge station. The path followed the roads quite a bit until, several miles down the riverside, it became a proper path. We crossed the river by the Rotherhithe foot tunnel. From here the path followed side roads through industrial areas until it emerged on the riverside again. When the Thames Barrier came into view, we all piled into a pub even though we had not quite reached our goal and then completed the rest of the journey to the barrier where the walk finished.

A great deal of celebration and photographs took place at the Barrier.

Like Richard Branson, I too was brought up thinking that we could all change the world. My parents were great visionaries and always told me if any man can do something, you can too. They also taught me to be generous in anything I do. Create win-win situations in all you do and do no harm.

My intentions are good even if the outcome is not always good.

So why be generous in the world when it is supposed to be a dog-eat-dog environment? This has never been my experience in my journey to date. I have come across people, even competitors, who have been generous with their time and ideas. You don't have to be generous with money, you can be generous with your time for example become a mentor, do voluntary work at your local authority. Give to charity.

My late friend Felix Dennis told me to be generous and he was generous to a fault. You never know where that generosity will lead you.

I know I would have never been successful in business without the generosity of my family, friends, my team and my foster carers whom I praise every day for the priceless work they do with children. They are the epitome of generosity having these children in their houses and are my everyday heroes!

Richard Branson writes about doing some good and I see this as much about being generous as doing good.

In my life and in my business, I am always thinking of ways I can help in any situation I come across. I ask myself how best I can add value to a situation and I feel many businesses have products and services which add value – they are being generous to their customers by finding solutions to their problems. Being generous is about doing something to make a difference.

Fraser Doherty states that most amazing business success

stories throughout history, are those of who started companies, not with the aim of getting rich, but with the aim of making the world a better place. So you too can do the same in your own way. I do this with my small charity, Vana Trust, which helps children and young people both in the UK and Africa.

I wrote some parts of this book in Cuba and while there I went to a Buena Vista show where I was able to see generosity in practice. The dancers gave their all with their generous spirit and smiles.

Generosity is everywhere you look. It needs to be unconditional where you don't expect anything back in return. I am always surprised how generosity goes round. Each time I am generous I find someone else is generous to me, completely unrelated and at a time when I need it. It feels like the universe remembers.

I have lots of examples of finding generous people, from competitors to suppliers, throughout my business journey, but the one that I believe enabled me to start up my business was from my staff themselves. Be generous. Lynne Franks always says give people more than they expect. When I started my first business, Imba, which was a therapeutic children's home, I had taken voluntary redundancy from Camden. Armed with an £800 redundancy package I decided to open this home.

I recruited and trained 10 residential social workers to work on the rota, providing 24 hour care to some of the most disturbed children in the UK. I didn't have wages to pay them, I didn't have a business bank account, never mind an overdraft facility. No bank in the High Street was prepared to open a business account for me as they didn't then know anything about children's homes or social enterprise.

So I decided to open up the challenge to my team of staff. I told them that I didn't have any money to pay them, but asked if they would come and work for me anyway. I couldn't pay their wages until I was paid myself from the local authorities placing children in my home. It was a huge gamble but I was so surprised then, and still am, that they agreed to this. I was a complete stranger to them but they believed in my passion and were generous in return.

They worked for six months under this arrangement and each time I got paid I paid them half of the hours they had done. I was humbled by their trust in me and when I was able to repay my debt to them in full, I did it with a good heart. These ten staff remained with me throughout until I transferred ownership to another company. To date, four of them still work with me. Looking back now, they should have been partners of the business. They funded my start-up and I remain grateful to them always. This is just one of many generous examples I have personally encountered.

In his *Building Social Business,* Muhammad Yunus talks about social business being a new form of capitalism based on the selflessness of people dedicated to solving social, economic and environmental problems that have long plagued humankind. I believe business leaders build their businesses not to amass billions of pounds but to solve a human problem.

I am sure when Bill Gates started Microsoft, he was trying to solve a problem, enabling the masses to have access to computers.

When Anita Roddick, my heroine, built The Body Shop, she was trying to save the environment. She used her persuasive passion to campaign as businesses are in a powerful position to contribute positively to the society in which they work. She summarised this in terms of power and influence – "you can forget the church and forget politics – there is no more powerful institution in society than business. I believe it is more important than ever before for business to assume a moral leadership. The business of business should not be about money, it should be about responsibility. It should be about public good not private greed."

Steve Jobs would have argued the same when he started Apple computers and later the Apple iPhone. He wanted to create a product which pleased the consumer. I believe he died still wanting to create that perfect user-friendly product. Again, another sign of generosity within business product creation.

In summary, try to be generous and see what the universe provides for you in return. I love Anita Roddick's advice: never be seduced into believing it isn't the role of business to tackle the big issues, because it absolutely is.

There are huge benefits from being generous varying from feeling good about yourself and offering help where needed or requested. The outcomes of being generous are long term in building relationships. Just giving unconditionally without expecting anything back is also beneficial. I am always amazed about how by being generous to others, people are so generous to me. You are giving out what you would like in return and the universe has got a way of giving back to you from people where you least expect it. Being generous is not only about financial giving but it is about giving other things like your time, goods in kind, exchanging ideas and being open to others as well as just giving money to someone to buy food, attend a course, clothing or start a business.

I know I would not have started my business without generous people around it. My friends and family were generous to me in allowing me to make my dream into a reality. I have many and varied examples as follows:

A stranger, my landlord Kenneth Wilson, was generous to me by allowing me to live rent free for three months in his house when I was setting up a therapeutic children's home, Imba. Here I was and a stranger saw my vision. I was honest and open with him that

I didn't have the funds to pay rent. He was so generous in allowing me to do this and I remain eternally grateful to him.

I then came across Triodos Bank and they were giving low interest rate loans for community projects. They wanted to loan £1,000 and they suggested I find 10 friends and family members to guarantee the £1,000 (at £100 each, as it was almost impossible to get anyone to guarantee as much as £1,000 in 1992 as it seemed quite a lot of money). I was able to find 10 friends and family members to do this which enabled me to get the £1,000 to start-up Imba. So, institutions can also be generous if you have a clear vision and passion about your work.

I believe I am a generous person because my family and friends are also generous people and have been generous to me throughout. Generosity is inbred and it feeds on generosity. So next time someone asks you for something just be generous and see what develops – it's just magic.

Key Messages

Be generous and don't expect anything in return.
Give unconditionally.
Generosity is everywhere.
Give your time, not necessarily money.
Give whatever you can.

Exercise

List things you could give.

Think of a time you gave. What did it feel like?

TIP TEN: HONOUR YOUR SUPPORTERS AND KEEP YOUR ENEMIES CLOSER

"In the practice of tolerance, one's enemy is the best teacher."
— **Dalai Lama**

"I defeat my enemies when I make them my friends."
— **Dalai Lama**

"Always forgive your enemies, nothing annoys them so much."
— **Oscar Wilde**

Marlow to Maidenhead

We started off with the stretches and salty baths which had become our morning routine. Today we were back to walking alone, just the two of us. The couple in Marlow who owned their house and also used it as a B&B had been very generous again. They had prepared a lovely breakfast and a huge lunch to take away – with lots of bottled water to keep us hydrated.

We went back to Marlow Bridge and proceeded towards Maidenhead. The river was growing in size with each bridge, making us feel we were making progress and nearing London, our final destination.

I am not sure where it came from but each morning we had new energy, felt refreshed and focused. Our spirits were upbeat and we were determined to keep going. My foot was now better but I was still being careful in my steps forward. I was hanging on to Thandi's trainers as I did not want the pain to return. I think by now she had forgotten they were her trainers. I saw her get up every morning and reach out for the hard heavy ones.

As the day progressed l got a text message from Marigold saying she would like to join us in Maidenhead and walk with us the next day. She had been so inspired by our story on the blog and on Facebook that she wanted to join us. l gave her the address of my friend's house where we were staying for the next two nights and looked forward to seeing her later at the Fat Duck. The Fat Duck was an experience l shall write about in the next book!

Marigold joined us at the Fat Duck that evening. She went straight there. As we got home we noticed she had come with flaxseed, bodybrush, nuts and molasses. We had not realised that all these ingredients were for a morning routine which l continued throughout the rest of the walk and still do today.

From my experience, when you start an enterprise you will get supporters from everywhere and some from the last places you would expect; like your competitors whom you would assume to be enemies. I believe you need to honour your supporters, as without them, you will not have a business. Work for me is about people, your relationship with them and is not really related to the product you are selling. You can't sell without the human input.

Daniel Pink has written *To Sell is Human,* which proves that without people you can't sell even the nicest of products.

I see my customers very much as my supporters in making my dream become a reality. They buy from me, recommend others, offer repeat business and help me grow my business. They offer feedback, give compliments, testimonials, concerns and complaints. All this support helps to develop your product or service. You can't grow without such input from your supporters. Cherish them. I see them as gold dust as they are indicators of what you are doing right and what needs adjusting.

Supporters also guide you or re-motivate you when things are not going well. They remind you of your passion, why you set up shop and demand that you keep going. Running any enterprise can be a lonely existence so get as many supporters as you can from the start. You will need them throughout. Sometimes I received support from the strangest of people. A few years ago I got a very painful right hand, I couldn't drive or use my hand for months. I felt disabled. At one point I couldn't even dress myself.

Then one of my previous carers heard about my illness in my office as I was at home. She was given my mobile number. One rule I have is that if any of my carers want my number they can have it. I don't have a private number, my personal life is intertwined with my work so I have one number. I want to be open, accessible and transparent to all those I work with. They are part of my life. I see them all as part of my family and am sure the same goes for them. Going back to the story…

She called me – I was surprised to hear from her as she told me about her own similar hand problem. I listened with interest and I was thinking she was phoning to wish me well, and here she was telling me about her problem. So I listened patiently. The call was difficult as it was hard for me to understand her as English is not her first language and I was in agony. I think English is her fifth language, which puts me to shame as I only have two languages.

Anyway, 30 minutes later she got to the point, she wanted to recommend a private doctor to me who had helped her five years previously. I thought, how kind. So she texted me the full name and details of this doctor with a message that she had already been in touch with him and he was expecting my call.

I was climbing the wall in pain and didn't know how I was going to call him, never mind visit him at his clinic in West London. But I got up out of bed, called him and he was able to see me the next day. I got up, took too many painkillers to tackle trains and the underground to West London only to be told I had acute Vitamin D deficiency as my black skin can't absorb the English sun!

He prescribed me three Vitamin D injections. One of them to be given then and there.

I could hardly walk when I got to this clinic, overdosed with painkillers. After my injection I walked out of that clinic feeling 100% better and have never looked back. So this call from one of my supporters helped me get better – it was a mercy call. I was so grateful for this call as not only did it enable me to know more about Vitamin D deficiency but I got better and was able to do the walk which was the inspiration for writing this book.

I love my supporters, they are always there no matter what. They love me unconditionally. They will support me with any grand ideas I come up with. They trust me to follow things through even when I make mistakes. They will offer a helping hand even when I fall down. They are just there when I need them making my life and entrepreneurial journey less lonely and frightening.

Sometimes supporters appear from nowhere. I come across an idea and I start thinking, oh I wish I could meet someone who knows more about this idea. Within days, sometimes hours, someone will present themselves who knows more and can help. So be careful what you wish for. Wish big, dream big, the supporters will appear and help you.

Competitors can be seen as enemies in the business world but I feel they are not really enemies.

From the start of my entrepreneurial journey I have always lobbied and campaigned to form support groups from my competitors. They helped me start up every business I have ever started. To date I am a member of such groups as BAAF Independent Fostering Agencies Forum and Fostering Network Independent Fostering Agencies Forum.

I have learned a lot from being a founding member of such groups. I learn about what my competitors are doing, share experience and practice for the development of my own agency. From these relationships we have had joint conferences on shared topics and ideas.

Some of these agencies have been set up by my own staff who have gone on to run their own agencies. I can therefore never see them as enemies. I keep in touch with them, mentor them and they always call me to cry on my big shoulders. You need to be open and share ideas because in return they always share useful ideas. It's all part of being generous, if you give, people will always give back.

I agree with Anita Roddick's advice, set your sights and skills on an idea, do the research, see what the competition is doing and then see how you can be different. Focus on what the competition doesn't have and promote that.

I have always done this throughout my entrepreneurial journey. My parents told me I was special and unique, so my business is about my specialness and uniqueness. Isn't yours also special and unique?

You need to stand out from the crowd. I have never seen myself as part of the mainstream. Anita Roddick also talks about being an outsider when you become an entrepreneur and went on to say entrepreneurs all suffer from hurry sickness, they have an abundance of energy and commitment. They create something out of nothing.

Each day I'm humbled by my supporters and I honour them for their unconditional support. They are committed to teamwork and working towards the same goals. They are there when things are down and when they are up. They celebrate with me all the successes and wins we achieve together. Without supporters you don't have a reflection of yourself, there is no internal dialogue to reflect how you are doing. We all need cheerleaders to keep us going, to validate that we are winning, check we are on the right track and that we are making a difference.

I remember my grandmother once telling me to, "keep your enemies closer", and I was too young then to understand what she meant.

As I started my business journey, I began researching my ideas. I looked at the potential competition as I saw them as enemies. But really they were not enemies and I learned a lot from them. I contacted them, visiting their homes and soon discovered they could teach me a lot about my business ideas.

Life lesson of the day:

With any idea you need supporters to expand the idea into reality.

Leonie's story as a walker:

I was 12 years old when Auntie Nyasha committed to this walk. I was hearing about the walk and I thought it was just for adults, until I heard that my cousin Ashley who is of my age group had done a day's walk and I thought I would give it a go. My Nana gave me a lift to Kingston Bridge and walked to Putney Bridge. I walked with other people but the people I knew there were Auntie Thandi and Auntie Nyasha. I enjoyed walking and felt happy to spend time with Auntie Nyasha. Thank you for allowing me to take part.

Key Messages

Honour your supporters.
Supporters are essential to any business and your personal life.
Competitors are not really enemies.
Learn from them and promote what they are not doing.

Exercise

Think of the supporters you have today, when was the last time you honoured them?

Think of ways you can increase your supporter pool

List people or organisations you see as competitors, enemies and next to their names make a note about how they can support you or how you can learn from them.

TIP ELEVEN: YOU ARE NEVER TOO OLD TO LEARN

"If you think education is expensive, try ignorance." — **Slogan on The Body Shop lorries**

"People don't care how much you know until they know how much you care." — **John Maxwell**

"Whenever I am caught between two evils, I take the one I've never tried." — **Mae West**

Maidenhead to Windsor

The morning was delayed by Marigold; we had to brush our bodies before a bath and drink flaxseed and water with molasses as well as warm water with lemon. Marigold slowly got ready and we were all soon spruced up and ready to walk.

Marigold was impressed by our resolve to do this walk and joined the spirit of it even when we were caught in showers. She stretched with us and watched in amusement when we climbed the fallen trees lying across the path.

It was wonderful having someone new and fun along the way with us. Her excitement was heartwarming. It was like watching a child in a sweet shop. As the day went by Marigold had caught the walk fever. She was hooked and cancelled a meeting in London as she decided to join us for the next day. We looked forward to and planned for another morning of flaxseed, bodybrushing, molasses and warm water with lemon.

Meanwhile we were now so fed up with restaurant food, we called for a homemade food supply from my sister who brought it with all the trimmings for the evening.

Charles, our host, arrived at his house to find it taken over by walkers and their visitors, bags and African food. Paul arrived soon after, just in time for the food. All in all we had a nice evening with friends and family, as my sister brought Chenai and the grandchildren in tow.

Life lesson of the day: Family are there for you no matter what. They love you unconditionally.

Marigold's story as walker:

I joined Nyasha Gwatidzo's "Walk the Thames with Me" adventure, aimed at raising funds for Vana Trust on days 11 and 12. We walkied from Maidenhead to Windsor on the first day, then Windsor to Shepperton on the second day, a total distance of just over 25 miles. We were blessed with very warm weather on the first day. Neither too hot nor too cool, perfect for walking. On my second day the weather was not so clement, it drizzled then rained for a while, which was still comfortable for rambling. It was a good experience for me as that is the reality of life; the sun does not always shine. One often experiences discomfort when helping others, such is the nature of sacrifice.

My original intention had been to walk just one day, expecting to last no more than 5 or 10 miles, but, once I joined, I enjoyed the experience so much I had no choice but to carry on. I just could not help getting carried along in the flow. Also, Nyasha and Thandi Haruperi's enthusiasm, determination and tenacity was infectious and so inspiring I stayed on for another day! Nyasha was limping noticeably from a foot injury by this time, but still carrying on without a care, such was her determination for raising as much money for Vana Trust as she could. I pleasantly surprised myself at my achievement.

I take my hat off to Nyasha and Thandi for walking such long distances in all kinds of weathers – 183 miles for Nyasha and 160 plus for Thandi. All in all, it was an exhilarating and truly memorable experience for me, a real eye-opener. It has fired up my passion for walking so much I walk anywhere and everywhere I can. Personally I feel it is so wonderful to support such good causes.

The highlights of the walk for me were the short picnics we took along the way in such beautiful scenery and in good company. It is amazing how much one works up an appetite when walking. We also picked wild plums as we walked along the Thames, gaining free and natural antioxidants from their rich Vitamin C content. I also overcame my fear of climbing trees by climbing a short one! Our backpacks were loaded with adequate supplies of food and water, which we thoroughly enjoyed. Another highlight was seeing so many beautiful boats and yachts along the Thames, most of them with fancy and exotic names like Desdemona and Innisfree. We also had the privilege of visiting Andrew's beautiful island home, the Sphinx on Pharaoh Island, which has a very interesting history which includes the famous Napoleon Bonaparte.

I was grateful for being sponsored by my local community, family and friends. I raised a reasonable amount for Vana Trust.

Each day brings so many learning opportunities. My best teachers are the children I have worked with over the years. The things they come up with in their innocence are so remarkable. Their stories teach me a lot about human nature and the instinct to survive no matter what has happened to them from varying degrees of abuse, neglect and loss.

Over the past thirty years I have learned a lot from them and I feel privileged to have their stories and hope my input touched them in one way or another.

I have always been a good student, wanting to learn from experiences, loss and separation, my mistakes as well as learning more formally through my degrees.

I also create situations within my team so that they continue to develop throughout their time within my company. The same applies to my carers. I want them to develop professionally and personally and, in return, this will empower and enable them to care for vulnerable children in our society.

One could say it is selfish but my learning and teaching of others is about improving myself always so that I can better help the children and their outcomes are improved. I like creating learning environments at my workplace. I offer university student placements and practice opportunities for social workers, as well as to psychotherapy and psychology departments from both UK and international universities.

Starting at school, I learned the basic things like writing and reading, but I also learned how to socialise, making friends and not so friendly friends. I consider myself to have been a good student, always handing homework in on time. I enjoyed school and learning opportunities plus passing exams.

As I grew up I moved from primary school to secondary school in a strange country. I had to negotiate differences, join groups of friends who had known each other since nursery. I learned how to manage being different and being marginalised.

This is how I developed my empathy for marginalised groups of people, as I know how it feels being some African girl plonked into a Yorkshire secondary school. This taught me to be more of an observer, which comes in handy. The culture shock showed me how to manage change, difference and how to seek support. I learned to ask for help. I stopped being shy so I could raise my head up to ask for help or the questions other students were too afraid to ask.

I use this skill to date in running my business. If I don't understand something, I ask questions, I research, google, read books, question experts until I get it.

During the economic crisis of 2008/09, I felt that, as a mother, I needed to understand the financial world so that I could learn how banks and financial institutions leave us in such a vulnerable situation globally due to our ignorance. So I am still reading, researching, educating myself about capital, who owns it and how the banks could get it so wrong. Six years later I am still learning and still don't understand any of it but from that reading I have set up a private equity fund to focus on social impact investment for women-owned businesses in Southern Africa – World Impact Capital.

It was a sense of outrage that drove me to want to do something about it. I was outraged about my own ignorance and wanted to educate myself and the outcome was World Impact Capital.

I feel enabling women to grow their business in the emerging markets is going to create jobs and in return they will feed and educate their children through enterprise. Look how children feature in everything I do, anything that will help children. I wanted to create something different from the charity model. So, from my own interest in learning – so that I didn't remain a passive economic idiot – I have created something which I will continue to learn about.

I will find people with the talent to explain this to me as I go along. I am also going to be learning how to do business in Africa, which will be a huge learning curve for me but it is where my heart is. I was born an African and will die one. This is one example in which I place myself in learning mode continuously, while at the same time doing business. I am always striving to learn more on subjects I don't know and in return I am teaching others about my experience, to improve their own practice, businesses and life experiences.

I always prioritise learning opportunities not just for myself but for my team as well, as the human brain is a sponge for information and learning. I have generous training budgets for both my staff and carers. I want to see them grow with me.

Twenty years after starting my business I was one of fourteen lucky people to be awarded a bursary to study at Cranfield Business School. I attended their Business Growth Programme. My friends and peers asked me why I attended such a programme as I was now a seasoned entrepreneur, what was I going to learn?

I told them I am always open to learning and if I don't learn anything, at least they can validate that I am on the right track. It was a great experience meeting forty-nine other business owners. I learned more from them than I did from the lectures and workshops.

Anita Roddick agreed we should learn from the Victorian philanthropists who endowed educational institutions, libraries and hospitals in their local communities and worked hard to improve the conditions of their employees. She went on to say they did this because they understood that a cohesive society is an essential foundation for business success and that their companies would thrive with healthier, better-educated and more productive people. It would be folly if, today, we didn't see the role that business can play in the development of human beings.

She foresaw the revolution for business schools becoming places where personal values and economic interests intersect.

Learning is addictive because it is joyful, and has always been for me since school days. It is also necessary for human evolution and this is why we are not extinct according to John Medina, a molecular biologist.

According to neuroscientist Gregory Burns, the brain chemical dopamine is released when people learn something new and exciting. Hence learning can be addictive, so you need to bombard your brain with new experiences.

I often explore things outside my own field or industry to enable me to see my world through a fresh view. You will become a more interesting person if you learn and share ideas from fields different from yours, try it.

When you lose the ability to think differently you lose the ability to inspire. Seth Godin was remarkable in his book *Purple Cow*. He thought of a cow but put a different spin on it and called it "purple cow". It's new, it's different and remarkable. Everyone he has taught or presented to will remember his novel and original idea. In learning new ideas, issues and continually trying to develop yourself, you are giving your brain a workout. If left alone the brain is just a lazy piece of meat, according to Gregory Burns.

I agree with Lara Morgan when she says people who have learning opportunities, and feel they have a development path, will stay and continue to add greater value to your business.

I offer both external and internal training for my staff and carers. Sometimes when one or two members of staff attend external training, they agree to come back and train us all on the subject – to everyone's benefit.

I always say, the day I stop learning is the day I die and I learn from varying situations that I come across each day but the best place I learn is in my work with children in care. I receive many profiles each day, telling stories of human beings, each one unique to that child and their circumstances. I learn about their suffering, the abuse they have suffered and how, despite all that, they are still alive and need caring and safe families to live with. They are survivors and they are my heroes and heroines.

I learn from foster carers with whom I work with each day. I am humbled by the priceless work they do with the children they choose to foster. They are strong, resilient and, of course, silent heroes working away 24 hours to do what I call "repair parenting" – trying to make it better for children so damaged by the society in which we live. I cry each day from these sad stories but I also enable myself to grow and learn about myself through reflection; and I find myself able to carry on.

As you remain open to learning, you carry on making mistakes and, oh boy, what an opportunity it is to be able to learn from mistakes. I see mistakes as huge opportunities to develop myself. I also learn from other people's mistakes. I read a lot of business books and from there I learn which mistakes not to make in my own business. I take out the messages which resonate with my values, to grow my own expertise.

I find I also learn from the least expected places or individuals, for example old childhood messages from my grandparents when I was young. These lessons meant nothing to me when they were being said nearly forty years ago, but today I find myself using them as a learning tool.

I have always been a good student, I did my homework on time. I was a teacher's pet as well as a pest. I would stalk them at lunchtime if I didn't understand a mathematical theory, for example, until they had explained. I wanted them to teach me and saw them as mentors.

I still am interested in learning from everyday life, as well as formal settings like schools, colleges, universities, and I have done it all with great pleasure. I believe this open attitude has led to success as I am humble enough to learn from every opportunity presented. Learning is all about growth and development. You are never too old to learn. Without learning we stop growing, which is detrimental to our wellbeing.

Key messages

You are never too old to learn something new.
Be open to learning and find learning opportunities.
Learning expands you.
Learn from everyday things.
Learn from your and others' mistakes.
Mistakes are a learning opportunity.

Exercise

List things you would like to learn to develop yourself.

What mistakes have you made and what have you learned from them?

TIP TWELVE: LISTEN! LISTEN! LISTEN!

Windsor to Shepperton

We were a bit more prepared for Marigold's routine in the morning so we started off on time. Paul hadn't had time to buy new trainers so he still had his, by now very torn ones, which needed to be tied up again with Thandi's extra pairs of socks.

This turned out to be a noteworthy part of the walk as we passed by the historical Magna Carta memorial in Runnymede before getting to Windsor, the seat of the royal family. Not that I am interested in the royal family but it was worth noting the tourists swamping the place when we arrived.

There is also a thriving tourist industry with shops selling anything royal. I am all for creating jobs so I couldn't knock it. We had lunch at the Riverside hostelry, which had a fantastic view. As we left, the waiter gave us free bottles of still water in support of our walk. Throughout the walk we met generous people like her and it encouraged us to keep walking, all watered and fed!

The walk started with four of us, Paul, Thandi, Marigold and I being joined by John at Staines. I had given John an approximate time when we would be arriving at Staines so he could meet us. John had wanted to join us at the start of the walk but developed a bad leg so wasn't able to do any walking up to then. We found

John waiting for us as we arrived in Staines and had a group breakfast in a community hall in the town centre.

Paul was walking at a faster pace than day three and was now more energetic. We stopped many times to stretch, sit down or lay down, as we meandered with the River Thames, taking our time as we spoke to passersby. It was just nice being by the water, sometimes alone and sometimes with the group.

Our host for the night was Andrew, who lived on an island on the River Thames with his new bride Emma. Andrew suggested he pick us up so we could do the last mile on his boat as we approached Walton Bridge. I had texted him our estimated time of arrival to give him enough time to come for us.

Marigold was petrified of this boat ride so she decided to walk a bit further and get herself nearer the island where she would only need to cross about 50 yards to get to the house. Having dropped us off, John had to go home.

The boat ride was such a relaxing treat, and took only ten minutes to land us at Andrew's beautiful house where we were welcomed with a swimming pool and all modern conveniences. It was really a lovely setting.

Zolisa and Peter arrived from London with our bags almost at the same time as Marigold. They stayed for photos and to look around the island. As Zolisa left, we decided we had more than enough clothes with us so we asked her to take the bags to my house in London. We selected the essentials we could carry for the rest of the walk. Paul refused to go home as he was enjoying himself too much, so he stayed until the end of the walk .

Thandi and I decided to relax in the hot tub before sitting down to unwind. In the evening when Emma arrived, we were treated to a lovely BBQ by both of our hosts.

All in all, a lovely ending to the day and we couldn't help posting some of the pictures. Next day we got comments on my Facebook page saying we were enjoying ourselves too much. For the kind of walk we were doing, people expected and wanted to see more challenge, tears, pain and stress but really we couldn't make it up.

The walk so far had not been the challenge l had expected.

The weather was good and I was in great company throughout the walk. I had met generous and wonderful people who just made the whole thing enjoyable. I was truly humbled by the experience.

Life lesson of the day: Appreciating how the other half lives!

Paul's story as a walker:

I joined Nyasha's walk as I was interested in the historic nature of the route. Starting at the source with only cows for company and a canoeist who popped up from the reeds to say he also enjoys skinny dipping. After a few days this changed into the 'film star region' around Shepperton Studios. After many more days we entered Henry VIII's domain, Hampton Court. Finally, after several more days we arrived at the City of London, passing Canary Wharf and the British Navy moored in the tidal Thames. I only meant to do one day, but started to enjoy it so much I ended up walking for nine days to the end.

Listening is a wonderful skill with huge benefits in your life and business. In his *The Virgin Way*, Richard Branson talks about combining note-taking with listening. Note taking is what I have always done and I keep these notebooks forever. In my work I am required to keep notes or diaries for 75 years so they may outlive me. I would agree with him about note taking aiding listening.

I use my notes as a reminder of agreed actions, even simple things like agreeing to send an email. A lot of people are impressed by my memory, they often wonder years later how I can remember specific details. It makes them feel special that what they told me was important enough for me to have listened and remembered.

Richard Branson sees listening as an ability to tune in intensely to what is being said. "That kind of wisdom such people manage to accumulate and dispense is directly attributable to their extraordinary listening skills." I see it as having ears behind your head, where you hear what's not being said. I agree that a skilled listener not only takes what has been said but will also hear what has not been said. When listening at this level you also pick up on body language, subtle undertones which reveal more than what is said.

Lara Morgan wrote a whole chapter in her book called *Shut Up and Listen*. She is really saying the more you shut up, the more you are able to listen as well as saying you can't speak and listen at the same time. I can't begin to stress the importance of listening.

I was fortunate enough to be born shy among extroverts in my family. This enabled me to listen to them and they never expected me to respond as I was too shy. This was a good training ground, which enabled me to develop my listening skills. As an adult I was lucky again to be given an opportunity to train as a therapist where we learned formally how to listen, even to painful and sad stories; how to listen to what is not being said; how to listen to the written word.

I believe magic happens when you listen properly – even to your own body, enabling you to look after yourself better. I am not always good at this and I pay the price with my health. Gut intuition also serves as a listening tool in that you should always go with what your gut is telling you and listen carefully.

If it doesn't feel right, then don't do it!

There are enormous benefits in listening and this varies from developing and creating new products, services, business if you listen to customers, staff, suppliers and the general public. It's strange how you get feedback about your ideas from various sources. People you would never expect to comment, and you need to listen even if you dismiss it later. It's all part of development.

I always listen to what is not being said, reading between the lines. This comes from being in tune with yourself and actively listening. It is a skill that you need to develop to properly process what is being said to you. Some of the most innovative ideas come from listening properly, then implementing them.

There is no point in listening to suggestions or feedback but not processing them or acting on what is useful and what is not. Most of the time I listen to things being said, digest and reflect on them – or do the opposite! Not sure if it is my entrepreneurial nature that is always on the side of rebellion. I was never a rebellious child but I make up for it now as an adult and in business life. Don't tell my mother.

Reflections

Reflection is about listening, reviewing what has gone well and not so well. From there you can adjust the course of your journey and reignite your determination to keep going. Reflection also gives you the opportunity to learn from feedback, be it from friends, professional peers, family or customers. There are people who carry on without reflecting on what they are doing. This can lead to lack of insight on the impact they have on other people.

It is also energy consuming to continue without reflection: I use reflection as a time to stop and take a deep breath before going on. This keeps us "safe" in the way we conduct ourselves by checking on ourselves every now and again, rather than running around like headless chickens.

Key Messages

You need ears behind your head.
You need to listen to what is being said, or not said.
Listen to your gut instincts.
Listen to your heart.
Learn to listen.

Exercise

List things that get in the way of your listening or enabling you to listen.

What do you do with what you hear?

TIP THIRTEEN: GET A MENTOR

Shepperton to Kingston (planned to Teddington)

The day started in style, taken again by boat to the mainland to start our walk. Our bags were all lighter and we weren't worrying any more about who would pick them up to deliver them to the next host.

John joined us. He was still struggling a bit with a bad leg but he was determined to carry on with us to the Thames Barrier finishing point. John was asked to carry the food as our bags had overnight clothes now, so he helped with the madness around him.

The walk itself became difficult as it got very hot as the day progressed. As we approached Kingston Bridge we found ripe wild plums which we picked and ate. Paul's shoes gave up in Hampton Court so he and John had to go and buy trainers while we rested in a riverboat cafe. We walked from the shade to shade, as we approached Kingston Bridge. We couldn't take any more of the heat so we agreed to end the day there instead of Teddington which was 1.5 miles away.

We had made very loose arrangements for where we were sleeping and, because of the misunderstanding, we had to find somewhere to sleep at the last minute. Thandi decided to ask her friend, Stella, if we could go and sleep at hers.

Stella warmly opened her house to us including our new friend Linda, another person who had contacted us and decided to join the walk after hearing about it on Facebook and following us online.

The day ended with us meeting Linda and eating more wild plums, which we had picked during the day. We had a bucket full of them.

Life Lesson of the Day: Plans can be changed.

Yemurai's story as a walker:

I had an incredible time walking a section of the River Thames. You do not realise how many places the River Thames influences, going through many small villages, towns and cities. This signifies how Vana Trust influences lives both in the UK and Zimbabwe. I am so proud of my Mum for doing this, waking up 16 days in a row, putting on trainers (regardless of the blisters), and continuing to walk. An incredible achievement, well done Mum, love you.

Lynne Franks recommends mentoring as she has always found networking and mutual mentoring with individuals come naturally to her.

Fraser Doherty talks about how useful it is to find a mentor to support you in your business journey. He found Kevin Darren, a local entrepreneur, who decided to take him under his wing.

Mentors are useful as a sounding board. They can be from a different sector to your own, but their experience and contacts will still be useful when starting up.

When I started my business journey, the word "mentor" was little used. I knew I needed someone to bounce ideas off, but didn't know that person was called a mentor. So I found ways of getting that support without the formal mentorship. Mentoring has become big business now but, as a start up, you might not have the funds to access mentors. However you can find ones from the Prince's Trust, Business in the Community or try a friend or family member.

I used my mother. She is an enterprising woman so I would talk to her about her experience, what worked for her and what didn't and today she is still my mentor. Just watching her doing her business inspires me. Because of my mother, we are an enterprising family and so my brothers and sisters are great sounding boards for me too.

The rest of my mentors over the years are really business leaders I admire. They range from Anita Roddick to Lynne Franks. They are really my role models as they never formally mentored me.

Having a mentor provides a lot of benefits including having a sounding board, an adviser, someone to bounce ideas off, someone's shoulder to cry on, someone to reflect with. When I started my business journey thirty years ago, the word mentor didn't exist, but I always knew I needed someone like this. So what did I do to create such a person? I created my own virtual mentors.

I read business books and follow profiles in the news on people I admire, such as Anita Roddick, The Body Shop founder. I attended conferences she was attending so I could get some of her tips, and feed off her passion to feed mine. So, she was my virtual mentor, without knowing me personally.

I also created a support group where I got all the owners of children's homes in South London to meet each other monthly at my house. I facilitated and hosted this and we were a group of ten women. We were competitors but also supporters of each other. These same women had been invaluable to me when I was setting up my own children's home. They had shared their mistakes, what I should not repeat, what works, their suppliers and so on.

This was created out of my need to reflect, to bounce off ideas and turned out to be the most important group I ever joined. I learned a lot, developing ideas with other women in the same business as me.

I am sharing these examples as sometimes when walking this lonely journey, you feel you need a celebrity mentor or even a lot of money to pay a mentor. This was not the case for me. My support group did not cost money and reading books and newspapers cost the price of the book. When I didn't have the money for the books I went to the public library or friends and borrowed them.

Mentors nowadays are everywhere. Lots of people are setting up as mentors and offering their services to wannabe entrepreneurs, so the choice is great. So don't be lonely in this journey. Find what suits your values, personality and what would be supportive to you.

There have been debates whether your mentor should be from the same sector as your own. I am open and flexible about this as I feel you can get a mentor who is not in the same market as support and structures are very similar. What is vital for me is having the same values as your mentor so that you are aligned in what makes you wake up in the morning. Having someone more experienced than you lets you learn from their mistakes and successes as you really can't do it all alone.

Running a business is a lonely journey and you need someone objective and supportive to make it less lonely. You need someone to keep you on track and accountable as you can easily become complacent being the founder of your own business. Mentors tend to be generous people in that they will make introductions within their own networks of useful people in your journey. Simple things like introductions to a bank which is helpful in your business can be useful when starting up.

Key messages
Get yourself a mentor.
Create support groups.
Seek out your role model.

Exercise

List people who you would like to mentor you, get their details, read books they have written.

Within your network, are there any people with whom you can set up a support group?

TIP FOURTEEN: BE ACCOUNTABLE AND ETHICAL

"*The final goal of any business activity and any business must show us how to be effective, is to create a world moral order – a world ethics network.*"

— Peter Koestenbaum

'*Whatever happens, take responsibility*"

— Tony Robbins

Closer to London, the logistics of getting back to Kingston Bridge were executed with great care in the morning as there were so many people joining me for the walk that day. We had all agreed to meet up at Stella's house. Linda was already there, John arrived at 8 am from his house nearby and my sister turned up with her grand-daughter Leonie, the youngest walker so far.

By 8:15am two cars were packed ready to go back to Kingston Bridge. Timing needed to be precise today as we also had Muni joining us at Teddington Bridge which was supposed to be the end point of the previous day's walk. Zolisa and Peter were to join us at Kingston Bridge but before they could even park their car they had to go back and help Zolisa's brother with a childcare crisis that had arisen.

By 8:45am we were all ready to walk. This time the six person team was made up of John, Thandi, Paul, Linda, Leonie and myself. It was a beautiful morning as we started with our routine at Kingston Bridge. We had to move quickly as Muni was waiting for us at Teddington. Thank goodness her train was delayed, so we didn't have worry about being late.

We had become a group now and we walked in ones, twos, threes and sometimes all together. It was lovely having new people on the walk. It was nice to have a member of the public, Linda, taking time to support me on the walk. It was a strange feeling as this walk was no longer about me walking alone. We joined up with Muni at Teddington.

Muni is a friend of a friend who had been inspired to take a day to walk with us – a fitness fanatic who did this route by foot or bike nearly every weekend. With Muni in the team, we were in safe hands.

Now, seven of us were trying to negotiate the Thames Path as we entered London. It was unbelievable – we had reached the outskirts of London and we were still going strong. No blisters, no broken bones or pulled muscles. Thandi was still pulling ahead, slowing down as and when she caught herself moving too far ahead, either on the phone or lost in her own world..

We were still standing, talking and walking at our own pace. As we walked, there were more trees of wild plums. This became a distraction for a while and we continued to pick them. We had even taken Stella a bowl full of wild plums, which were just ripe and sweet straight from the trees. All good, healing stuff.

We passed Kew Gardens by lunchtime and saw people very much into their own thing, sitting in gardens, having picnics and ice cream. It was odd to see people just getting on with their daily lives fully unaware of our walk.

As we approached Putney Bridge the water was rising and part of the Thames Path was flooded which meant we had to climb the rails to cross about 20 yards of water. This was the high point of the day, as we had to cross the flooding to continue.

Photos and videos were taken to mark this experience amidst lots of laughing. It was such a joy to be part of it!

Paul was still enjoying the walk. He was happy with his new shoes, which seemed to be supporting his feet. At the end of each day I thought he would have given up, but he stayed on!

We ended the day at Putney Bridge, said our goodbyes to Muni and Linda who needed to return home to their young children as her nephew couldn't cope with them. Linda left reluctantly as we carried on, but she promised to return for another day once she had sorted out her children.

Women multi-tasking and struggling is still the order of the day. We ended up at Blain's with Bev, she had been one of our biggest cheerleaders throughout the walk, with texts and comments on Facebook, despite herself being ill with pneumonia. Blain treated us to dinner at his local and gave us somewhere to sleep for the night in Battersea.

We were now in London – it was unbelievable. I had told my staff at Banya last time I was in the office that next time I come into London it would be on foot – unimaginable at the time, but here we all were now.

Life Lesson of the Day: So near but yet so far, can see the light at the end of the tunnel.

Muni's story as a walker:

All I can say really is that it was great walking with such amazingly beautiful ladies. Nyasha, Thandi and Linda are just beautiful and of course we had the youngest walker on the walk, Leonie, Nyasha's niece who gave us all a run for our money. No doubt she will grow up to be a phenomenal woman.

There is no better way to spend time with great ladies than walking along the beautiful river Thames, with its beauty, oh and not forgetting the high tides which saw us having to improvise walking under the bridge in Barnes!

The men were great too! I managed to catch a few conversations with both of them. I still laugh when I think about the crossing at Barnes Bridge! How neither would join us in our adventurous crossing but instead walked a good distance back to join the road.

The second half of the route we walked that day remains quite special to me. Everytime I walk from home (Putney) to Barnes (I do this walk regularly) I can't help but smile as I recall walking for Vana Trust. I enjoyed every minute of it and will definitely do it again if the chance arises.

My grandmother inspires me! With little education, widowed in her early 40s, she spent sleepless nights crocheting 'doilies' and travelling to South Africa to trade. She travelled to Zambia in the heat of war in the late 70s to take guardianship of her younger sister's children. Her sister had died post birth leaving a two month old baby and 7 other children. She successfully brought back all the younger children to Zimbabwe and raised them like her own. Today, in her 80s she remains amazingly generous, kind and just fabulous and the best grandmother in our world....just phenomenal!

Anita Roddick writes about persuasive passion which is a process of auditing, being accountable and transparent in your personal life and in business. Even large international companies now see the value of "good" and ethical business practices as being good for business, society and environment according to Lynne Franks. So what are the values which drive you both in your personal and professional life? I include my values in any business plan as I feel my life is entwined with my business and must be, to succeed.

Values are my route map, my guidelines in how I want to live my work and home life. They are more my internal belief system. You therefore need to align your values and ethics within your business plan. My values include respect, taking responsibility, and treating others reciprocally like you would like to be treated. We all have different values and priorities. My priority values drive my own passion, I seek to ensure they are aligned in all I do in personal and professional work.

In being accountable you need to know that the only person responsible for your own success is you. You therefore need to own up to your own actions and decisions. You also need to learn very quickly how to overcome obstacles and organise.

I feel blessed as I don't have the disease of procrastination. I call it a disease as it is disabling and can paralyse the procrastinator.

They do say that people make a judgment or decision about you within seconds of meeting. I don't make decisions within seconds, but I make them quickly as I find it painful to remain indecisive. I feel paralysed until I make that decision. Of course I look at the pros and cons of things or ideas, but I do decide.

I remember talking to my mentor about this once and explaining that whatever decisions I make were right at the time even if it later turns out to have been a mistake. My intentions at the time were right so it wasn't really a mistake. After all, you can always learn from those mistakes. Oscar Wilde's "experience is the name we give to our mistakes" often comes to mind.

Being accountable is about making decisions, owning them and standing by them. It is about making assessments of the situation and making a judgment and running with it. One might ask how you remain accountable and ethical in such a ruthless business world where there are constant challenges like new regulations, new friends or frenemies, new competitors.

There are several approaches that help me. Reflecting back on my values and my passion, I read inspiring books which recharge my batteries. I attend conferences, seminars, and hang around with friends and family who reground me. I knit or go for a walk, which gets me into a meditative state and relaxes me again. I focus on what is important. You need to find ways that enable you to remain accountable, and not cut important corners.

Running a business or a family does take its toll, both physically and mentally. So you need to take time to look after yourself. It's really about being accountable to yourself. As a woman and mother, I know it's easy to forget about oneself as there are so many demands from children, family and professional life.

You need to take care of yourself to keep the ship running. Find a way to recharge those batteries so you can remain accountable. It's easy to slip if you are not feeling your best.

I swim, knit and walk as a way of recharging myself. I also take regular holidays to get away from the daily emails and calls which can get in the way.

Delegation is another tool I use to help me remain accountable and focused. I look at tasks that need doing and ask myself continuously, am I the best person to do this task? If not, then I delegate it to someone else who does it more effectively than me. I also make those I delegate to accountable so that they get things done with clear instructions and deadlines.

When my children were young I had to delegate some childcare to my family i.e. sisters, cousins, mother-in-law to support me. For example every school holiday my mother-in-law had my eldest daughter to stay which freed me to focus on my business without worrying about pick up times from school. You need this level of support. Lara Morgan says you need a world-class nanny and if you treat her as such, she will be core to your success and give you the freedom to achieve every other possibility. I wouldn't disagree with this, as my family were core childcare supporters, world-class supporters whom I treasured equally.

I find being organized also helps me to keep focused and accountable. I don't really work well when surrounded by chaos or without plans, goals and diary. I write all my things to do in my notebooks and never go anywhere without them, even on holidays. It's quite refreshing to tick off the items.

As for my diary, it changes all the time, it has its own life but I always say if it's not in my diary it won't happen, making me accountable. I feel half of the battle is showing up so, once it's in the diary, I will show up.

Being organised also gives me confidence that I will complete the tasks in hand. Being accountable is about starting a task, following up the challenges that come my way and seeing it through and taking credit for the mistakes and successes along the way. To do this you need to be organised, focused, and you need supporters to assist you. I see being accountable, responsible and ethical as being interrelated. You can't do one without the others.

Anita Roddick talked about business – just as in life, we can't avoid moral choices – after all, the future depends on it. I believe being ethical and responsible is the only way to do business and the only way to lead your life too.

You should really be led by your values. Sometimes your ethical values are questioned; then you go back to your core values. What drives you? What motivates you? Refresh, evaluate and audit them as you go along.

I always admired Anita Roddick for her value auditors report, which was public and too transparent at times but she did it because she wanted to learn and improve practices at the Body Shop.

Most businesses would thrive from that level of ethical commitment. It's good for business and the community.

Anita Roddick was talking about corporate social responsibility before it became fashionable. Now there is a whole industry on the subject. For me it's about how to implement these in a meaningful way in your life and business and not just a mask to cover up unethical practices. It's a big request for business, but consumers are going to force the issue.

In setting up any business you need to bear in mind the responsibilities that come with it. It's a huge responsibility. Just like being a parent, it is uncharted and there are no manuals. You have to take on the impact of your business operations from the way you treat staff, suppliers, customers, stakeholders as well as the impacts on the social, physical and political environment.

If you don't want to be accountable, then please don't start up a business or become a parent. There are so many people relying on you from day one, that you need to step up and be accountable throughout as the buck stops with you. This is a shocking realisation to many people, including myself. My business is all about my passion for children. I got into business by mistake, due to my passion. I never woke up one day and said, I want to be a businesswoman. I woke up one day when I was four years old and realised that I liked babies and this passion remains with me.

So there I was, following my dream of wanting to help children and soon woke up with the realisation that I was running a business. Imagine the shock one day when a twelve year old walks into my children's home and asks my team who is in charge? I had to do a double take with myself as I had never thought I was in charge, two months into opening a children's home. So I shyly raised my head above the parapet and answered that I thought I was.

Children are so good at cutting through bullshit and getting to the point. They are excellent educators and I learn each day from them. I learned from that question over thirty years ago. I remember it as if it happened yesterday: I was in charge, I was accountable and I had to up my game!

I use my values as foundations to accountability in business and in life. When in doubt, I go back to them, to check whether I am still in alignment with my own values. I ask myself, would I like to be treated like that, as a measure of how I treat others. This keeps me accountable and ethical in all I do.

I feel privileged to be able to run my business so I need to remain true to my values and accountable to my stakeholders and supporters as well as my competitors. They keep me on my toes.

Above everything else, I am accountable to the children I am privileged enough to be asked to care for. This is the most humbling of all and I am in some sense accountable for the childhoods into adulthoods of children of the most vulnerable people in our society. How else can you be but accountable for such precious people's outcomes?

I also have a legal duty to remain accountable, as in forty or fifty years time these children can ask what I did to help or support them while they were in my care. What a huge responsibility! So I also need to check and reflect on being accountable to myself and to put my hand on heart that I did what I did with all good intentions.

You therefore need to surround yourself with people who will keep you grounded, accountable and ethical in your life. These can be mentors, family, friends, advisers, customers or stakeholders. You need all of them.

Key messages

Be accountable in all you do.

Be ethical.

Remain true to your values.

Exercise

Who are you accountable to in your life and in business?

TIP FIFTEEN: MANAGE ENDING, SEPARATION AND LOSS

"Everything that is good has to come to an end." — **Chaucer**

Putney Bridge to Tower Bridge

Morning glory started in Putney Bridge. Here were John, Paul, Thandi and myself outside Putney Anglian Church Cafe as we waited for another walker to join us, aunty Mo's daughter Labisi.

We missed Muni, Leonie and Linda who had joined us the day before but we were joined by Labisi, who brought with her a new spirit and energy for the walk. We were walking in a daze really by then, not believing where we had walked from or whether this was more a dream than reality.

I thought I would be in pain and feeling tired but I was full of energy and felt as though I could fly, never mind walk. Thandi felt the same, we really did not want to stop, we now knew the next day was the final day. Just one day to go.

We were still reflecting on this as we passed Blain's flat again, having returned to the starting point where we had finished the day before. Bev's cooked breakfast and treats as we got underway made the whole challenge beautiful and bearable. But was this really a challenge?

Bev recovering from pneumonia walked with us through Battersea Park. She really wanted to join, even if only for a short stretch as she wanted to do her bit with us. She had to soon part with us as she really wasn't well. She had got herself into the t-shirt and the pictures, and bid us goodbye!

We crossed the bridge over to the North Embankment towards the Tate Gallery where we had another coffee break, looked around and moved on to the South Bank. This was really a difficult stretch of the walk for me, there were many people in the way, making it difficult to focus on the route.

At the Royal Festival Hall we met with Thandi's daughter, Molly, who couldn't get over how suntanned her mother was from walking in the British summer sun. It was great to meet up with her, to remind us of grandchildren encouraging us along the way.

We continued on the South Bank and headed to Tower Bridge which was our end stop for the day. The crowds remained in our way but we forged on with sheer determination, we were counting steps to the final destination. It was so good to walk at our own pace, not rushing as we didn't have a set timetable to reach our destination.

It was a really strange feeling, I was thinking about what I was going to do after the walk, I was already missing Thandi, who had delayed her journey to Harare for this walk. She was leaving in a few days time so I wasn't going to have her around for doing the stretches or even comparing notes about how we were feeling.

I am not that good at goodbyes, so I was starting to prepare myself to say goodbye to the routine of the walk, Thandi and all the walkers that had followed me. We reached Tower Bridge by 4pm and went into City Hall for tea, only to be told it was closed.

We found a cafe nearby and sat down for a quick bite before heading for London Bridge to get to Chido's where we were sleeping for the last day. Being so close to home, Thandi changed her mind and went to sleep at her own house which was understandable. It was good to sleep separately as tomorrow would be our last day away and this was an emotional preparation. We agreed to meet the other side of Tower Bridge for our usual 8am start the next day.

Life lesson of the day: Loss and separation are inevitable in life.

I struggle with endings both in life and business. How do you end things you do with all your passion, commitment and determination?

I don't do things by halves, either I am in or I am out, I am a woman of extremes really.

On this walk, as in any journey, things all have to come to an end. I had to think of ending it in a positive way, with tears, but happy tears, as I'm an emotional woman.

I had to reflect on what I have learned and what I have gained on this walk. The same applies to about 50 years of my life, 30 years of that as an entrepreneur. How do you reflect on such an enormous journey?

All the lessons, the mistakes, the opportunities, the missed opportunities, the tears and the joy, the sadness and despair. I am left humbled each time by each and every one of them.

These are all gifts even though at the time they didn't feel that way.

I have found even things like moving house very challenging, never mind ending a relationship. With a divorce, I felt I was going to die with distress but I lived to tell the story.

With my team of staff I cry each time they resign even though I know they have to seek new ventures. I hardly sack anyone, as I feel worse than they do for doing it.

It's all about fear of rejection. Loss and separation, endings are all about rejection. In ending something you are rejecting something old and starting something new. We are all scared of the unknown but this is what drives us.

I always remind myself I am taking a risk each morning I awake, as I don't know what the day will bring, so I get up, take a deep breath and start again.

As my business grows and I plan for my exit, I am always feeling scared of rejecting my "baby". How do you prepare for such a thing emotionally?

It is heartbreaking to consider but I remember thirty years ago a bank manager asked me why my business plan didn't include an exit plan. I remember thinking, what an odd question. Why do I need to have an exit plan when I am just starting my business.

Today I think how insightful he was and now understand why I needed such a plan as you do need to plan this carefully.

Use all your mentors, enemies, supporters, advisers to support you with endings. Attend all workshops available on how to plan your exit. Do all these to lessen the burden, for me it's a painful process.

At the end of it you have to let it go and try something else. They do say when one door shuts, another one opens!

This is very true of my own business experience. I left my children's home to start a fostering agency and I have never looked back. It was perfect timing with huge opportunities. I didn't know at the time but I followed my gut instincts supported by my passion and market research.

In her *Business Nightmares*, Rachel Elnaugh talks about how Red Letter Days ended. She ascribes her loss of passion to Red Letter Days, which is now seen more as a big uncontrollable machine.

I suppose business is like life with messy bits, challenges and rewards. Some people can't cope with the messy bits because they can't see a way to solve the problem and it leads to the business failing, closing and ending.

As a woman I wonder if I am too emotionally attached to my

business, "my baby", to see logical solutions. I often say I am too soft for this rough business world and prefer to do it my way by following my gut instincts and emotions.

Lynne Frank has written a whole book on the subject of doing business the feminine way.

Everything good has to come to an end but how to do this in a positive way?

I am not very good at endings. I just want to keep going, as endings are painful.

Saying goodbye is difficult but I have to find ways of managing this.

It is a form of rejection when you have to end something, even if it is planned and well prepared for.

Focusing on the positive things that have happened normally helps. Listening to feedback given and finding ways to action any of the feedback that you found useful.

I find myself coping, by focusing on what the next plan of action is.

Key Messages

Endings, separation and loss are difficult.
Prepare for endings.
Seek support around endings and loss.
Focus on the way forward to making endings less painful.
Look at the positive bits of the endings.

Exercise page

List losses, separations and endings you have experienced to date and next to it write a note/comment on how you managed it.

TIP SIXTEEN: CELEBRATE YOUR SUCCESSES

"Success is knowing your purpose in life, growing to reach your maximum potential, and sowing seeds that benefit others." — **John Maxwell**

"I owe my success to having listened respectfully to the very best advice, and then going away and doing the exact opposite." — **G K Chesterton**

"If you want to reach a goal you must "see the reading" in your own mind before you actually arrive at your goal." — **Zig Zigler**

"It is high time the ideal of success should be replaced with the ideal of service." — **Albert Einstein**

Tower Bridge to Thames Barrier

Last day of the walk, the main question for me was, how do you end such a walk?

I had confused feelings, varying from feeling happy that I had achieved my goal and the challenge was coming to an end, but also sad that I would not be walking again with all the people that had joined me. I didn't know whether to laugh or cry. I got to Tower Bridge with these thoughts on my mind wondering how the day would end.

I had to take a deep breath and face more new walkers joining me at Tower Bridge. Mutsa, Dave and some HSBC Staff were joining me with Paul, Thandi and John still hanging in there. Linda was coming back to do her second day as she had sorted out childcare. Cathryn was going to join us at Greenwich.

So all these logistics had to be managed with care, I couldn't afford to get stressed on the last day. Both Mutsa and Thandi kept us waiting as they were running late but I was not to be stressed. The walk started after 9am which was late but we didn't care, we were still on track and the goal was in sight.

The River Thames meanders round the Limehouse Basin, Canary Wharf and up to Greenwich. We met up with Ben from HSBC at Canary Wharf all suited up for work but he had been given time out to walk with us some part of the way. His other colleagues couldn't wait as we were an hour late getting to them.

We continued walking, enjoying nuts and raisins Mutsa had brought us as well as Linda's fruit salad. We were kept well fed and watered. We crossed the river via the underground tunnel at Greenwich and met up with Cathryn who was waiting for us at Nandos. We had a great lunch there but I was also anxious to get to the end.

Cathryn was ready to start her walk and support us to the end. She was in awe of us having arrived and that we had sixteen days to date. Our group was now complete for the day and we were to be met by Zolisa and Peter who were taking me from the barrier to the farm.

Thandi was being met by a friend who was taking her back to her house in Croydon. As we approached the barrier Tawanda (a Zimbabwean Olympian), called to inform us that he was in the area and would meet us there.

Cathryn had blisters and was struggling with her feet. We were sympathetic but also shocked and couldn't quite make sense of it as neither of us had had blisters throughout the journey.

I applied blister cream which I had carried throughout just in case. I thought Mutsa would have blisters too as she had got new trainers especially for the walk.

Tawanda joined us from about 200 yards from the barrier and took so many photos. I reached the barrier just behind Dave and was so relieved and pleased. Zolisa and Peter were already there taking pictures of the end and then the remaining walkers. Thandi was not way far behind me. Again I was not able to express how I felt – happy or sad. We spent time reading some facts about the River Thames and comparing the map and relating it to the journey we had just finished.

It was unbelievable, more group, then single photos of just me and Thandi were taken and we had to say our thanks and goodbyes. Thandi left with her friend and they gave Dave a lift to Croydon.

Cathryn, Peter, Linda and John were given a lift by Tawanda to the next train station to return to their respective houses.

Zolisa and Peter gave me and Paul a lift back to the farm. I thought I would sleep en route but I was still hyper from the walk. Reaching home after seventeen days on this journey was great and refreshing. I was ready to sleep in my own bed and cook my own food. I had taken the rest of the week off work to rest, so went to bed feeling good about my achievement and still wondering when the pain would appear.

Life lesson of the day: Don't start something you can't finish.

Mutsa's story as a walker:

I joined Nyasha and co at Tower Bridge on the last leg of her 180 mile journey from the river's source to the Thames Barrier in aid of Vana Trust, a journey that took sixteen days, walking everyday. Nyasha was joined at different points of her journey by friends and family. Paul and Thandi Haruperi were the constants of this epic walk. Thandi doing one hundred and sixty miles! The journey was made special by everyone who supported the walk, from those who donated money, food, washing facilities, accommodation, companionship, and so on. At a personal level I'm very grateful to all of my North East London NHS Foundation Trust Acute Services colleagues who sponsored me for a total of £530 and some family members who donated £60 bringing the overall total to £800. They would all be pleased to know I DID IT - the whole 12.65 miles– no limos, no champagne, but sheer determination to do something good in brilliant company. HSBC even sent some of its staff to walk with us in between meetings. Amazing. I commend Nyasha for her selflessness and determination and spirit of giving which was demonstrated by everyone who gave. I thank you all.

It is often said that success doesn't lead to happiness, it is happiness instead that creates success.

I believe having passion and purpose in life creates happiness because you are doing something with a purpose. Therefore within that success, happiness can be created.

So how do you go about celebrating small or huge successes.

I buy myself flowers as waiting for a someone to do it is a bit painful as it rarely happens.

My ancestors had great ideas of celebrating things: Harvests and rainfall with lots of music, drumming and alcohol, so how do I do this in London which is so far away from my ancestors. Find ways that are appropriate to your situation and have fun in the process.

I agree with Rachel Elnaugh that success is just a case of being able to hold your nerve. You should therefore find a way to release this nervous tension by celebrating.

Lara Morgan talks about celebrating in style, whether small or large, it all counts. This varies from a card saying thank you to a packet of jelly babies or a holiday in Barbados for a week with her staff!

Anita Roddick talks about managing success. She felt time spent managing success almost kills the entrepreneurial spirit which supports you. Keep this spirit by having several experiments or projects going on. That's experimentation at its best, when it is covert and when you can beaver away, polishing the experiment, shaping it until you have developed the idea. Then, and only then, you grin and move on.

There is no time to rest on your laurels to keep the entrepreneurial journey going in your celebrations of success.

My brain moves a hundred miles an hour all the time, always

thinking of new products or new practices to better the outcomes for children. While celebrating one event I am already thinking of what comes next.

My friend Clive once called me a "bottomless pit", always on the go, too many ideas and he felt tired just listening to me, never mind carrying out the actions. I could have taken offence to being called a bottomless pit, but I knew exactly what he meant.

People often find this level of energy disconcerting but I celebrate my gift in having the energy and brain to think and the stamina to act.

Lynne Franks talks about recognizing our gifts and delegating the rest. Just as I am not able to procrastinate, I don't like dwelling on success. I feel the need to move on quite quickly.

I think this is due to my shyness and not being able to beat my chest for too long. I hate attention focused on me as my success is a by-product of my passion and my team. I can't do any of these things without other people supporting me. I know my family and my teams over the years have supported me unconditionally to enable my dreams to come true, so yes, we need to celebrate this in style like Lara Morgan suggests.

Lynne Franks talks about constantly planting seeds as well as picking the blooms.

Celebrating your success is really validating your efforts, energy and contributions to society. People do this in so many different ways, it doesn't matter how you do it, so long as you do it.

I am not very good at this myself, maybe because of my shyness, I don't really want to show off or be the centre of attention. However, I know celebrating is nothing to do with showing off so I need to keep focusing on that instead.

Celebrations are affirmations that you are on the right track, rewarding yourself as success breeds success. In celebrating the success, you are opening up for more success.

In Shona culture it is also about honouring your ancestors, thanking them for being along on the journey.

On reflection, sometimes I feel I struggle to celebrate my successes no matter how small, as I take it for granted. I feel humbled by it. I think I was born successful and with abundance hence there is nothing special about my little successes.

The issue is really how do you honour these in a modest way or a way that feels comfortable to you.

I am learning, as I get older, how to do this and started with simple things like buying myself flowers and going to spas. In the office I buy flowers every week for all to enjoy and celebrate our success.

I understand success means different things to different people.

Key Messages

Take time to celebrate your success.
Celebrate your success no matter how small.
Don't forget your supporters in your celebrations.

Exercise

List your current successes and note how you marked them or not. Go back to those you didn't celebrate and comment on how you will celebrate next time.

REFLECTIONS

A week after the walk

I was back to work five days after the walk. I had continued my routine of stretching each morning and night, soaking my feet in ice and hot water each day. I followed Marigold's advice, brushing my skin and drinking flaxseed water first thing in the morning.

I had washed Thandi's socks and returned them to her but was still feeling attached to her trainers so held on to them for a while. I had cranial treatment, Bowen treatment and massages including one at The Athenaeum Hotel spa with Thandi. This was sent to me by Mutsa, the ever helpful cheerleader. My knees remained stiff and painful when going down the stairs but the stretching routine helped. I had rested and was thinking of another challenge for 2015!

On reflection I think the reasons for having done this walk were achieved. I was healed, feeling a lot better within myself. I had raised awareness of Vana Trust and had strangers supporting the cause and I had also raised over £8,000 for Vana Trust. Asked if I would do it again, my answer would be ... not the Thames but another challenge. This was a one-off!

Three months after the walk

I was at Victoria Falls, Zimbabwe with Thandi, writing the first draft of this book and planning the next walk with her. Thandi does not help really she just encourages no matter what crazy ideas I come up with.

She is a great supporter and generous with her time.

USEFUL RESOURCES AND CONTACTS

Thames Head Inn, Tetbury Rd, Cirencester, Glos, GL7 6NZ
Contact: 01285 770259

Upper Chelworth Farm, Chelworth Rd, Cricklade, Swindon, SN6 6HD
Contact: 01793 750440, Mrs Hopkins

Cambrai Lodge, Oak Street, Lechlade on Thames, Glos, GL7 3AY
Contact: 01367 253173, Mrs Titchener

Rose Revived on the Thames Path, Newbridge, Witney
Contact: 01865 300221, Mrs Lockley

Oxford Thames Four Pillars Hotel, Henley Road, Sandford on Thames, Oxford, OX4 4GX
Contact: 01865 334444

Oasis Private Care, 85 Hanney Rd, Steventon, Abingdon OX13 6AN
Contact: 07910 31457, Mrs. Hancock

52 Blackstone Road, Wallingford, Oxon, OX10 8JL
Contact: 01491 839339, Mrs Enid Barnard

Oak Tree B&B, 76 Oak Tree Road, Marlow, SL7 3EX
Contact: 01628 475340, Sheila/John Budd

REFERENCES

Axline, V (1990) *Dibs in Search of Self: Personality Development in Play Therapy* – Ballantine Books

Barclay, L (2010) *The Unauthorised Guide to Doing Business The Duncan Bannatyne Way* – Capstone

Boyle, D (1999) *Funny Money: In Search of Alternative Cash* – Harper Collins

Branson, Sir R (2006) *Screw It, Let's Do It: Lessons In Life* – Virgin Books

Branson, Sir R (2014) *The Virgin Way: Everything I Know About Leadership* - Portfolio

Dennis, F (2007) *How to Get Rich* - Ebury Press

Doherty, F (2011) *SuperBusiness: How I Started SuperJam from My Gran's Kitchen* – Capstone

Dyson, J (2000) *Against The Odds* – Textere Publishing

Elnaugh, R (2008) *Business Nightmares: When Entrepreneurs Hit Crisis Point* – Crimson Publishing

Franks, L (2000) *The Seed Handbook: The Feminine Way to Create Business* – Thorsons

Godin, S (2005) *Purple Cow* – Penguin Books

Handy, C (2006) *The New Philanthropists* – William Heinemann

Henderson, H (1996) *Building a Win-Win World* – Berrett-Koehler

Hill, N (2007) *Think and Grow Rich* – Marketplace Books

Johnson, Dr S (1997) *Who Moved My Cheese?* – GP Putnam's Sons

King, B (2010) *Bank 2.0* – Marshall Cavendish

Maxwell Magnus, S (2003) *Think Yourself Rich: Discover Your Millionaire Potential* - Vermilion

Morgan, L (2011) *More Balls Than Most* - Infinite Ideas

Parkes Cordock, R (2006) *Millionaire Upgrade* - Capstone

Piketty, T (2014) *Capital in the Twenty First Century* – Le Capital au XXI Siecle

Pink, D (2014) *To Sell is Human: The Surprising Truth About Persuading, Convincing, and Influencing Others* – Riverhead Books

Pryce, V (2015) *Why Women Need Quotas* – Biteback Pub

Ratner, G (2007) *The Rise and Fall..and Rise Again* - Capstone

Roddick, Dame A (2000) *Business As Unusual* – Thorsons

Thompson, Y (2014) *7 Traits of Highly Successful Women on Boards* – Panomapress

Yunus, M (2010) *Building a Social Business* – Public Affairs Books

ABOUT THE AUTHOR

Nyasha started her social entrepreneurial journey with a £800 redundancy package and abundant passion for children. She was a founder and campaigner for introducing independent children's homes and fostering agencies to work in partnership with the public sector.

As a black African woman, she faced discrimination in her journey but sheer determination and passion saw her develop a successful social enterprise.

This book is full of tips she has learned over this period and she hopes it will inspire you to do whatever you are determined to do, guided by your own passion.

Nyasha is a founder and executive director of Banya Family Placement Agency (an independent fostering agency).

Over the past twenty years she has won and been a finalist of many business awards, varying from social enterprise of the year to businesswoman of the year for her work. She has also won charity awards for Vana Trust, a children's charity she founded.

Biographical Info

My personal and business journey: major landmarks, losses and successes

1960s Born in a rural village, Wedza, Zimbabwe. Started babysitting for village family from the age of 4

1970s Arrived in UK, Sheffield on a freezing cold February morning

1983 Finished A Levels and came to London to study chemistry. Lambeth Women in Mind.

1983–1990 Treasurer of Zimbabwe Women's Network

1985 Married Matthew Poe in Zimbabwe and London

1986 My first daughter born in London

1987 Got my degree in Chemistry and enrolled to do a PhD at Imperial College London

1987 Started Hoxton Health Collective – first ever GP Practice run as a collective

1988 Completed literature research for my PhD thesis but decided solid chemistry was not my passion

1988-1990 Started and completed Gestalt Therapy and Contribution Training at Pellin Institute, London

1991-1993 Fostered for Westminister

1992 Started first social enterprise – Imba, a therapeutic children's home. Separated from Matthew

1994 Second child born

1995 Third child born

1995 MA in Therapeutic Childcare from Reading University

1996 Set up Friendly-ear, an online counselling and therapy service

1996 The Guardian selected me as one of the top 100 influential women in London

1997 Diploma in social work from Open University – qualified as a social worker as I needed this qualification to start my next enterprise – Banya, an independent fostering agency

1997 Banya started with four Imba staff who become my first foster carers for Banya

1998 Won my first business award from the Federation of Black Women Business Owners at Hilton Hotel, Park Lane, London

2000 My father died. Imba transferred ownership

2003 Founded Vana Trust, a charity that helps children in the UK and Africa

2006 Attended Cranfield's Business Growth Development Programme

2007 Anita Roddick died – I cried and still mourn her today

2008 Married Paul in Zimbabwe, then London. My mother got 15 cows. I'm sure I am worth more than that!

2009 Won Lambeth Social Enterprise of the Year Award

2009 My first grandchild was born. Soon became my best friend

2009 Marked having placed 1,000 children with Banya

2010 Won Businesswoman of the Year from Sue Ryder

Foundation

2012 Nominated for Zimbabwean Businesswoman of the Year by Zimbabwe Achievers Awards in London

2012 Vana Trust won a community award from Zimbabwe Achievers Awards in London

2013 Nominated for Businesswoman of the Year by South African Chamber of Commerce

2014 Walked the length of the River Thames for 16 days for Vana Trust

2014 Started World Impact Capital, a social impact fund to assist women's enterprises in the SADC region to grow their businesses

2014 Became Fifty

2014 Felix Dennis died – the world lost a very funny man

2015 Visited Cuba, a country I had always admired and wrote more than half of this book whilst I was there.

Nyasha Gwatidzo
nyasha.gwatidzo@banya.co.uk
+44 (0)7713 794163

BANYA

Banya is an independent fostering provider. Our fully supported foster carers look after children and young people placed by local authorities. Banya supports foster carer households nationally from Hampshire to Durham .

Hundreds of children and young people have benefitted from placements with our foster carers since Banya was founded in 1997. We aim to provide a high standard of foster care for a range of children and young people.

Banya has developed specialism in placing sibling groups, unaccompanied children and young people from overseas, children with special complex needs and teenagers with emotional and behavioural difficulties.

If you think you can take up such a challenging and yet rewarding job and become a foster carer, please do not hesitate to call us at Banya on 0845 402 7657 or email info@banya.co.uk or visit our website: www.banya.co.uk

VANA TRUST

"Enriching the lives of vulnerable children and adults by promoting self-esteem and developing confidence and skills through education, commitment, encouragement and support"

The "Walk With Me" book was written by the founder of Vana Trust, a UK registered charity (1105276) set up in June 2004. "Vana" is the Shona word for children and the charity was established with the aim of advancing good health and education for children and young adults in Africa and the UK .

St David's School Project at present funds school costs of nearly 100 children affected by HIV/AIDS at primary and secondary schools. Our support for a child sponsored by Vana Trust continues after leaving St. David's school with further education or training if that child so desires.

Vana Organic Farm Project is an eco-friendly 8 acre farm set up with the aim of unlocking the potential of children and young adults with special needs, behavioural and emotional problems within the tranquility of an organic farm. The farm opened in September 2009 and is located in Buckinghamshire, UK .

All profits from this book will go to Vana Trust. If you would like to get involved or donate please call us on +44 (0)1844 237146 or e-mail: info@vanatrust.org.uk or visit our website: www.vanatrust.org.uk.

CONTACT ME

When I am not walking I spend my time running Banya and also mentoring others starting their business journey, running workshops, seminars, speaking both nationally and internationally, talking about my journey so far and entrepreneurship, in particular, social enterprise. I also run workshops on fostering with the Pellin Institute.

All these are about inspiring others to achieve their own success, tap into their own passion and purpose and enable them to make their own dreams become a reality.

To find out how, by walking with you, I can add value and create a win-win situation for you and/or your team on your own journey, please contact me via my websites: www.nyashagwatidzo.com or www.walkwithme-books.com or e-mail: nyasha@nyashagwatidzo.com or nyasha.gwatidzo@banya.co.uk

Like my Facebook page https://www.facebook.com/nyashasbook and follow me on Twitter https://twitter.com/WalkWithMe_NG

Made in the USA
Charleston, SC
11 October 2015